31 Investment Opportunities You NEED to Know About

Learn about the basics of stock market investing, forex, day trading, real estate, penny stocks and even marijuana stocks (Beginners Guide)

Written By Kemp Joseph

purposes only. All effort has been executed to present accurate, up to date, and reliable, complete information. No warranties of any kind are declared or implied. Readers acknowledge that the author is not engaging in the rendering of legal, financial, medical or professional advice. The content within this book has been derived from various sources. Please consult a licensed professional before attempting any techniques outlined in this book.

By reading this document, the reader agrees that under no circumstances is the author responsible for any losses, direct or indirect, which are incurred as a result of the use of information contained within this document, including, but not limited to, — errors, omissions, or inaccuracies.

Table of Contents

Introduction

I have always had opportunities to invest money. In the beginning, I was investing without any experience or knowledge of what I was doing. I have nothing to show for these investments because they were not able to yield any form of passive income.

I spent several years of my life working day jobs, and I have been lucky enough to have a situation where I earned $150,000 annually working 40 hours in a week. During this period, I had access to loans, so I was buying cars and living a life of luxury. It was the kind of life I dreamed about.

With enough money to spend, I was smart enough to put a sizable chunk of my monthly salary into a savings account. Watching my savings grow used to gladden my heart – I was happy I would have something to fall back on in case of any unforeseen circumstance.

Well, it came as I imagined. I got tired of the job.

I realized that money is not a great motivation to keep a job. So, I quit my job and went back home to make plans for my next move.

Looking back on how I handled the situation, I made many mistakes. I was missing a lot of things in my life. Although I had a savings account, it wasn't bringing in any reasonable interest. I also learned the hard way that investing in cars is not a smart move. While I made some money selling my cars, the value on each vehicle had depreciated over the few years I owned them.

My rent was burning through my savings fast, so I moved to a cheaper apartment. I was young and naïve, so you can't fault me for wanting to get the best out of life. Before I could think of a good plan, I was back looking for another job. So much for wanting to chase my passion.

My huge turnaround came when I met a senior citizen relaxing at the park. Trying to start a conversation to make him feel at ease, we talked at length on various life issues and how there have been lots of changes in the world. In his quest to convince me of certain things that have remained the same, he brought up stocks.

He was explaining the stock market and how trading on the stock market still feels like the old days. Seeing it as an opportunity to improve my knowledge, I started asking many questions. It was the first time I was exposed to boundless opportunities lying in wait for me to act.

I didn't miss this opportunity. I took my time to perform extensive research for half a year. By this time, I had started living a frugal life, only spending on necessary things. By the time I got my next job, I had put in what was left of my savings into profitable stocks.

It was my first step, and I didn't look back since then. I continued to expand my portfolio and diversify my investments until I was able to build a reasonable return from these investments. I didn't visit any school to learn how to invest. I was only lucky to meet an expert at a time when I needed one the most.

This book contains a collection of various investment opportunities that you can quickly get into if you also want to live a life of financial freedom. I consider it my way of giving a similar help that I received when I was at the lowest point in my life.

Reading this book is an easy way to learn about several investment opportunities that are open to you if only you knew about them. With the knowledge you will gain from this book, you will be able to determine the right investments that will help you build the life you are striving for.

If you want to be successful in making profitable investments, you should not limit yourself to reading this book.

According to John Donne (1624): "No man is an Island, entire of itself: every man is a piece of the Continent, a part of the main."

The sooner you realize that you must not stop in your quest for knowledge, then you will achieve much more than you imagined. If you are ready to make the most of your time and money, then read on to discover various profitable investments that can change your life for good.

Chapter 1: Investments

What Is an Investment?

The process of purchasing an item or asset that will appreciate or yield a steady income is known as investing. These items or assets that are purchased are referred to as investments.

An investment may also be any monetary asset that has a possibility of yielding profits when sold at a future date. The investment covers the purchase of assets such as real estate property, stocks, and bonds.

There are two main types of investments available. These are the:

- Growth investments
- Defensive investments

Growth Investments

Investments that have the possibility of experiencing an increase in their original value are growth investments. The price of these investments reacts to the up and down movement of the markets.

Shares and property investments are common growth investments.

Shares

Shares are also referred to as equities. Investing in shares provides an opportunity for the value of your initial investment capital to increase over the period of investment. In addition to the increase in value, shares also pay a steady income which is known as dividends.

In comparison to other assets that investors can purchase, shares usually yield higher returns.

Property

Since long term investments in property can also lead to an increase in the value of these properties, they also fall within the growth investments category. As a growth investment, they also carry the risk of losing their value if the market moves in a downward direction.

Property investments can either be direct or indirect.

Defensive Investments

These types of investments have a lower risk in comparison to growth investment options. The main aim of a defensive investment is to yield steady income regularly.

Defensive investments include cash and fixed interest investments.

Fixed Interest Investments

This type of investment will offer investors a steady return on their investment at a lower risk level. The lower risk will also result in lower returns on investment.

Bonds are the most popular form of fixed interest investments. They are defensive investments because they offer lower risk and also yield interest from the company or government issuing the bonds. Similar to cash investments, it is easy to sell bonds.

Cash

Another popular defensive investment is a cash investment. Cash investment opportunities include the high-yield savings account that banks offer. In comparison to other forms of investments, the returns on cash investments are usually much lower.

The benefits of a cash investment include the regular return on investments and the ability to protect your capital investment.

Why Should You Invest?

To Create Wealth

Creating wealth is a goal that is very difficult to achieve if you only depend on your day job. The easiest way to define wealth creation is your ability to grow your money. There are different ways to increase your money, and these methods revolve around investments.

These investments may be in the form of stocks, real estate, or starting a business. The most popular investment vehicles that aid in wealth creation include bonds, certificate of deposits, stocks, real estate investments, and more. Investing in these vehicles over a long-term period will provide returns that will build up your wealth.

While starting a business is a significant investment, it usually requires a lot of time and effort if you hope to gain returns.

You Can Gain High Returns on Investments

There are different methods people adopt when they decide to hold money. The most popular way is to store the money in a savings account. It is an approach which offers minimal risks.

The only issue with a savings account is the low rate of returns. Due to the low price of returns, it is possible for individuals to lose some of the money in the savings account due to fees and inflation.

By investing money in stocks, real estate, or investment funds, it is possible to gain access to higher rates of returns. Although there will be times when the returns on investments may be low, the profits are usually much better than what a savings account offers.

It Helps in Diversification

Diversification is crucial if you want to gain financial freedom. Investing your money provides access to various tools that aid in assets diversifications. Investing enables you to understand that having all your money in just one sector can lead to financial issues in the future.

As an investor, it becomes easier to understand why your money should be split into cash, real estate investments such as your house, hard assets such as precious metals and cars, as well as investments that bring in more money such as stocks and bonds.

It Offers the Benefits of Compound Interest

To simplify what I mean by compound interest, I will define it as having your money work for you.

To explain how compound interest works, consider you have $1,000 that you use in purchasing a fund that offers a steady average return of 5% per year. After the first year of investment, you will earn $50 on the initial investment of $1,000.

In the second year, you still earn the same $50 on the $1,000 investment, but you also make $2.5 on the $50 profit from the first year. Now your money has increased from the initial $1,000 investment to a total of $1102.5.

Although this growth may appear to be slow in the early years, it becomes much faster in the later years.

As a result of compound interest, you continue to get more money without making any significant effort. It is merely your money working for you to bring in more money. If you can grasp the concept of compound interest, you will have a more solid grip on the power of investments.

You Minimize the Chances of Making a Mistake in the Future

Learning to invest now will help you understand the basics of investing. While it is necessary you read a lot on investing before taking the first step, practical experience will always provide more lessons.

Investing when you have just a $1,000 is better than waiting until you have $10,000 available. Making mistakes that lead to the loss of $1,000 will provide many tips on how to better invest $10,000. On the other hand, if you lose $10,000 the first time you invest, it will be challenging to try any investment opportunity in the future.

Lower Tax Rates

In comparison to the tax, you pay on money you earn from working, the tax on investments is much lower. State income tax, Medicare, federal income taxes, and social security are some of the taxes that apply to the working class. Also, local taxes may also apply depending on where you live.

As an investor, investing in a 401(k) or IRAs allow your money to grow for an extended period without being affected by the tax. If you can get a Roth IRA, you can also withdraw all your money when you retire without paying any tax.

In most cases, you can pay as low as 15% in taxes on long-term capital gains. If you feel this is a lot, it is crucial that you understand that it is almost half of what you are required to pay in taxes as a worker.

Taking advantage of this simple tip is one of the secrets to become wealthy.

Retire Early

Sometimes, becoming rich may not be the primary goal of investing. It can just be to have enough money to sustain yourself and your family without any source of income. That is why people have a 401(k) account.

It is essential that you understand that you will not be able to work all your life. At some point, the option to get money in exchange for the hours you put in will become unavailable. At this point, you need to be financially secure.

Diversification of your investments will help build a portfolio with income that can sustain your needs every month. To achieve this, you need to start investing while working. You don't want to get to that retirement age and realize that you are not well prepared financially.

If your returns on investment become high enough to sustain your needs, you will have the opportunity to retire early. You can then start living the life you desire.

It is Easy to Become an Investor

There are lots of reasons why it is easy to preach

investment to people of different age and financial standing. To invest your money, you don't need to be super rich or super smart. You also don't need to dedicate all your time to become an investor.

If you have just the beginner knowledge of investing, then there are numerous investment ideas for you to choose from. As a worker that is merely planning to retire with enough money to live a good life, then a 401(k) can be a suitable investment. Some of the benefits of this investment are the absence of a minimum requirement and the opportunity to earn free money from an employer matching program.

Investing in index funds also offers an easy way to make money from investing without expert knowledge.

It Becomes Easy to Support People

There are lots of people that need support. They may be family, friends, manufacturers, or businesses. Having a good investment portfolio will provide the money you need to be able to support those you care about.

You can choose to become a philanthropist if that is one of your dreams. You can also become an angel investor to various businesses that get your attention. When you start to assist others in reaching their goals, it becomes easier to feel good about yourself.

To Beat Inflation

Inflation is the increase in prices of commodities and items with time. It is a simple concept that has a considerable effect on the possibility of an individual paying a higher price for the same thing later.

Consider a case where there has been a 5% rise in the price of a car in one year. If the car cost $1,000 initially, its cost after inflation will be $1,050. On the other hand, putting your money in a savings account with a 2% annual interest will give you a total of $1,020 after a year.

The above calculation implies that you will be short $30 on the payment of the car. It means that you are experiencing a loss in purchasing power amounting to 3%.

For smart individuals that choose to invest their money, the returns on investments can be much higher. In some cases, the annual returns can be about 7% or more. If you are getting a 7% returns annually, you will be able to beat inflation by at least 2%.

Access to Free Money

One of the most popular forms of retirement investment is a 401(k). For individuals that work in a company where a 401(k) is available, an employer matching program may also be available. Under the program, you will receive an amount equal to a percentage of your contribution from your employer.

You are only eligible for the money from your employer if you are active in your 401(k) investments. To further explain, an employer may offer to match the first 5% salary contribution from an employee's salary towards their retirement savings. It implies that if the employee decides to save 5% of their salary in their 401(k), then the employer will also place an additional 5% of their salary in the same account. The extra 5% is not part of the original salary.

Depending on the generosity of your employer, you may enjoy a more significant percentage on the matching program. It is free money that is available to you if you are willing to invest in your retirement.

Some companies may not offer a matching program to their employees. It is easy to know where you stand by asking the HR representative in your company.

Achieve Your Financial Goals Faster

An important reason for starting a savings account is often to reach a target financially. The goal may be necessary to purchase a new house, car, or to pay for college tuition. Although having a savings account is beneficial, it can take a longer time to achieve your goals using this method.

On the other hand, investing your money in the right way can get you to your goals much faster. It is often due to the higher rate of returns you can enjoy from investing.

Essential Steps to Take Before Investing

Check Your Finances

Investing your money is excellent, but it is crucial you are investing at the right time. Before investing, the first step is to ensure you have an emergency fund. Since most investments tend to be long-term investments, it is essential that you have enough money to sustain your needs for at least three months after making investments.

Having a checking account and a savings account is also essential. While the checking account should be able to cover your monthly living expenses, your savings account should be prepared for costs that are not regular. These include house maintenance, car repairs, phone replacements, and various other expenditures.

If you are barely getting through the month on your paycheck, then investing may not be an option. Although it is an excellent consideration, it is not the right move at your current position.

Identify Your Tolerance for Risk

The type of investments that make up your portfolio depends largely on your risk tolerance. Everyone has a different risk tolerance, and it is essential you determine yours. As an individual, you may enjoy activities with high risks such as mountain climbing while others may prefer to read a book by the fireplace.

As a result of risk tolerance, certain individuals remain unaffected by a considerable drop in the value of their investments while a slight drop will significantly affect the emotional state of others. Different factors affect the risk tolerance of certain individuals. The type of investment, the net worth of an individual, age, and experience usually influence the risk tolerance.

With investments, the higher returns come from high-risk investments while low-risk investments usually offer lower yields, to minimize the impact of high-risk investments, diversification plays a vital role. Investors can just spread the investment capital over several high-risk investments, so they do not lose all their money on a single investment.

The best form of investment is a portfolio that offers minimal risk and high returns.

Learn the Basics of Investment

Investing has become more comfortable with technological improvements. Nowadays, it is easier to connect to brokers from anywhere around the world and invest without in-depth knowledge.

Nonetheless, having a basic knowledge of

investing is still significant. To increase your chances of making the right decisions and choosing the best investment option, you need to understand the simple investing terminologies.

Various websites teach the basics of investing while you can also gain access to multiple books from successful investors. These will give you information on different investment strategies, differences between the various investment opportunities, diversification, and more.

Determine the Investment Style That Suits You

Your investment style is usually a collection of the methods you use in controlling your investments. There are various investment styles available to investors when building an investment strategy.

Investors may choose an investment style that is conservative or aggressive depending on their risk tolerance. A conservative investor is one that has a lower tolerance for risk. These investors usually have an investment style that focuses on value investing, passive management, and large-cap companies.

On the other hand, aggressive investors usually take more risks. The investment style will often consist of active management, growth investing, and small-cap companies. The growth style and small-cap companies typically imply that there is a potential for rapid growth and high-returns from the company in question.

A portfolio of an aggressive investor will usually consist of a large amount of equities investment. The conservative investor will have a portfolio consisting of a small amount of blue-chip equities and a large amount of fixed-income securities offering low-risks.

What Are Your Goals and How Much Will it Cost?

Establishing your investment goal is another critical step to take. The goal is often beneficial in determining the best types of investment to select. The purpose of an investor will usually be determined by the needs of the investor and their background.

As a young man of 30-years earning a steady income working, your investment goals may be determined by your desire to pay your kids' college education and live a comfortable life. On the other hand, an individual that is close to retirement may be more interested in investing for retirement. Therefore, a lot of young people can invest in cryptocurrencies while a lot of older individuals will focus more on an IRA account.

The safety of your investment capital also depends on the costs of investment. There are certain investments with expenses that may affect the returns you get. In most cases, individuals that choose an active investment style will usually incur more cost than an individual using a passive investment style.

Investments like mutual funds may also have costs of operation and load fees that investors need to pay. Using a stockbroker will also result in costs in the form of commissions.

Selecting an Advisor or Broker

The commission they charge, their reputation, services they offer, performance, and frequency of communication are some of the things you need to consider when selecting an advisor or broker. It is an important decision that will also depend on your risk tolerance and the amount of time you have to monitor the investments.

There are brokerage firms that you can work within a situation where you don't plan on running your investment account on your own. Some minor issues with brokerage firms are the minimum requirements to open an account and the high cost of the services. Nonetheless, they usually offer excellent facilities and expertise that can be difficult to match.

Pick Your Investments

The best part of starting as an investor is often the time when you decide to build your investment portfolio. Your portfolio will consist of all the investments you select depending on your investing style. In this case, diversification and asset allocation play vital roles.

Asset allocation and diversification involve splitting your money and investments into cash, equities, and fixed-income. It is better to lose on stocks from one company in a portfolio consisting of assets shared between ten companies.

When selecting investments, you should choose your investments to cut across cash, stocks, real estate, and bonds investments.

Things You Need to Avoid When Investing

Although investing may seem like a simple task, there are several mistakes that people make before and after they begin investing. Learning about these mistakes early can help you avoid them so you can make more informed decisions.

Here are some of the mistakes you need to avoid:

Procrastinating on When to Start

There is nothing worse than procrastination. It has a more significant impact when it has to do with gaining financial freedom. In investing, it is better to start early. The longer you delay, the more difficult it becomes to take the risk of investing.

If you have missed the opportunity to start investing in your twenties, then the best time to start investing is to start now.

Not Taking a Step to Invest

Everyone has fears. Many people doubt going into a venture they do not have complete control over. In truth, investments can sometimes be unpredictable. Individual markets may experience massive growth this year but may also suffer an enormous setback in the next year.

No one can assure you that you there will be no down periods during your investment period.

The only thing I can say for sure is that if you don't take a step, there will be no chance for a better future.

Your Inability to Take Advantage of Money That is Coming Free

There is nothing better to hear the word 'free.' The same applies when investing. One of the best sources of free money when investing is an employer that offers to match your 401(k) contributions.

If you don't take part in such a program, you may end up losing all the benefits that your employer offers. Several employers offer to match the amount in your 401(k) up to a certain amount. Another advantage of these programs is that they are usually tax-free.

Short Term Investing for the Money You Don't Need

With most investments, the yield usually gets better the longer they are invested. If you will be making short term investments, it is crucial you make sure you will need the money within a short period.

If you have money you will not need for a long time, then you should make long term investments. Don't make the mistake of making a short-term investment with money you don't need. As humans, it is easier to spend money that is within our reach on things we don't need now.

Not Paying Off Your Debt Before Investing

If you want to invest with the hopes of enjoying the returns on your investments, then it is essential you pay off your debts. It would be best if you start by paying off debts accumulated on your credit card. In comparison to the annual return rate on investments, the annual interest rate on credit cards is usually much higher.

It means that if you have the exact amount of money to pay off your debt and decide to use it to invest; the amount you will earn in one year will not be able to cover the credit card debt after one year.

On and Off Trading

When you are on and off in your investments, you are finding it difficult to commit to investing. As a result, you will be more of a short-term investor. The main issue here is that you miss out on the benefits of long-term investments.

As a long-term investor, you can reap massive rewards over the period you invest. If you are inconsistent with your investments, you are likely going to lose most of your profits when you consider the fees you must pay when you need to reinvest.

Taking Excess Risks

As an investor, there are certain investments that you need to avoid. An investment opportunity that offers returns that seem too good to be true usually has high risks. It is also essential that you avoid using all your investment capital on a single investment.

Investing in the Wrong Things

When you are young, there are lots of things you may consider to be significant investments. If you are spending a lot of your money on collectibles, comic books, or lottery tickets, then you are making a huge mistake. You need to understand that if things were that simple, then complicated markets like the stock market and forex market wouldn't be necessary.

Taking the Safe Approach

I am not advising you to take excessive risks in this case. All you need to do is to have a portfolio that consists of long-term stock investments when starting at a young age. At this point, the salary from your day job can cater for your monthly living expenses.

As you get older, you can start buying more bonds and other investments. These can provide an income for your daily living.

Chapter 2: The Stock Market

What is the Stock Market?

The marketplace whose primary purpose is to allow investors to buy and sell stocks with ease is the stock market. Stocks trading can be over-the-counter or on a stock exchange platform. A stock is a fraction of a company which signifies the ownership of that company. In this regard, the stock market is a marketplace where investors can buy into or sell the ownership of a company in the form of assets.

For rapid and effective economic development, the stock market is a necessity. It is a marketplace through which capital is readily available to companies. The public provides the capital in the form of investments.

How Do Investors Trade Stocks?

Over-the-counter trading and stock markets are

standard options for trading stocks. The stock exchange is a marketplace that is regulated by a government body like the Securities and Exchange Commission (SEC). Through the regulations of the stock exchange, the market operates effectively while investors can avoid becoming victims of fraud. Some of the major stock exchanges include NASDAQ and the New York Stock Exchange (NYSE).

Trading stocks over-the-counter (OTC) is also an essential form of stock trading. Any stock that is unable to meet the criteria for listing on a stock exchange will usually trade OTC. A market maker or dealer is responsible for handling the stocks in this method of trading. One of the downsides of OTC stocks is the unavailability of reliable information regarding the stocks. It is a result of the lack of strict regulations.

Stock Market Indexes

A stock index shows the overall performance of stocks using a collection of different stocks.

Different stock market indexes are focused on tracking and revealing the stock market's overall performance.

These indexes are also available for trading by investors. They exist in the form of futures contracts and options.

Some of the major stock market indexes include the Standard & Poor's 500 Index, NASDAQ Composite Index, Dow Jones Industrial Average (DIIA), Hang Seng Index, Financial Times-Stock Exchange 100 Index (FTSE 100), and the Nikkei 225 Index.

Concepts of Stock Market Trading

The "bull" and "bear" are the two most significant trading concepts in the stock market. When a stock market is described using the term "bull," it implies that the market is experiencing an increase in stock prices. When the market is experiencing declining prices of stock, it is described as a "bear" market.

The bull and the bear markets both offer opportunities for investors to make profits. Short selling is a trading method through which investors can make money off a bear market.

When short selling, an investor will decide to go to a brokerage firm to borrow stocks. Since the investor does not own these stocks, only a brokerage firm can supply the necessary stocks. The investor borrows the stock with the intent to sell the stocks. The investor is selling the stock after analyzing the markets and determining that the price of the stock will soon experience a decline.

As soon as the stock prices decline according to the investor's prediction, the same amount of stocks which the investor sold can be purchased at a lower price. The difference between the amount the investor sold the borrowed shares and the cost of repurchasing the same number of shares is the profit.

Stock Investment Styles

Value Investing

It is a form of investment style in which investors search for stocks that are currently trading below their book value so they can purchase. Stocks that are undervalued on the stock markets are often a result of an extreme reaction from the market to the news. The response of the market to news will often cause a movement in the price of stocks which is not an accurate reflection of the long-term performance of the company offering the stocks.

A value investor will see this price movement as an opportunity to purchase the stocks of a company at a much lower price than their actual value. If you are seeking to invest in stocks over a long-term period, then value investing is usually more profitable than growth investing.

How Do You Identify Value Investment Stocks?

Irrational reactions from investors result in undervalued stocks. As a value investor, your goal is to use this irrational behavior to your advantage. Identifying stocks that have been affected by the irrational behavior of investors is quite easy. Just look out for the following features in a stock:

- Price-to-earnings (P/E) ratios below average

- Dividend yield above average

- Price-to-book ratios lower than average

Shares offering a great comparative value are usually those that value investors choose to purchase. Discussing value investing is quite easy, but it is also tough to implement.

The ability to correctly analyze the value of a company using the data available is difficult to master. Therefore, two different investors may have different opinions regarding the same company.

In addressing issues that may arise due to a wrong analysis, a margin of safety is always included before a value investor will finally move on to purchase the discounted stocks.

How value investors go about their analysis usually varies making this form of investment subjective. The approach of individual investors is to use the cash flow estimates and potential for future growth in assessing a company. There are also others who only have an interest in the current financial standings of the company.

Regardless of the approach or analysis that value investors employ, they all have one rule that guides their investments. This rule is merely the purchase of undervalued assets. To make a profit on the acquisition, they wait for the asset to reach its fundamental value.

Growth Investing

Growth investments are usually based on the potential growth of an asset. Companies that have earnings with a projected growth that is a lot faster than other companies within the same industry is usually the target of growth investors. These investors are known for investing in growth stocks.

The capital growth strategy is another common name for growth investing. The aim of getting the best capital gains is a reason for this name. Most growth stocks are usually stocks of emerging companies. With these companies, their success provides a great opportunity to earn massive returns. Like with all investments, high returns on your investment are only available with equally high risk.

Common opinions regarding growth investing and value investing place them at two extremes. While value investing involves investing in a company with underpriced stocks, growth investing involves overpriced stocks.

Evaluating the Growth Potential of a Company

The emerging markets and companies with high growth potential form the targets of growth investors. In meeting the financial and capital goals of a growth investment style, both the subjective and objective approach is necessary. The historical financial performance of the company is also essential for growth investing.

- The factors that enable growth investors to choose the right investments include:

- Revenue and cost control by management

- Forward earnings growth of the company

- Historical earnings growth

- Five-year growth potential

- Business operation style

Vehicles for Growth Investment

Implementing a growth investment strategy is achievable through different means. These means include:

- Blue chips investments

- Purchase of recovery shares

- Investments in emerging markets

- Investments in small companies with excellent growth potential

Types of Stock Investments

Dividend Stocks

Investing in dividend stocks is one of the best ways to earn steady returns on your investments. A dividend stock is also a dividend-paying stock. Through a dividend stock, an investor can receive a share of the profits made by a company.

Another benefit of a dividend stock is the opportunity to enjoy from the periodic increase in the dividends from the company. Most companies that offer dividend stocks are usually mature companies with financial stability. If the cash flow of a company remains consistent over the years, it reduces the volatility of their stock prices. As a result, they can provide dividends.

A lot of people invest in dividend stocks since it is a low-risk investment opportunity.

How Does it Work?

To invest in dividend stocks, The first step is to connect with a broker. You can look for an online broker that meets your requirements and then create a brokerage account. Once you have the account, it is essential that you fund the account with your investment capital.

Since dividends are a portion of a company's earnings, research is also vital. Your analysis should identify different companies that pay dividends, the value of the profit, and the consistency in paying dividends. You may also find tools from your online broker that can assist.

Before you receive your dividends, the Board of Directors of the company will need to approve the payment. Important dates regarding a dividend are as follows:

- Declaration date: It is the day on which investors will learn about the intent to pay dividends, time of record, and payment date from the Board of Directors.

- Date of record: On this day, a company will determine the investors that qualify for the upcoming dividends. These are usually the investors that are eligible as a holder of a record before the ex-dividend date.

- Ex-dividend date: This date is a form of deadline. It is a date before which investors must own stock to qualify for the next dividend payment. It means that if you buy a stock after the ex-dividend date, you should not expect to receive dividends on the upcoming payment date.

- Payment date: On this date, the company will pay out the dividends to each shareholder.

To make the most returns from investing in dividend stocks, it is crucial that you reinvest your dividends for a certain period. An increase in the frequency at which you receive dividends also improve your returns.

A simple example of making money from dividends

If you decide to invest in 200 Facebook shares selling at $150 per share. Your total investment will be equal to $30,000. If the stocks pay an annual dividend of $2, your profit after owning these shares for a year will be similar to $400.

The above is just a simple one-year example. You can hold dividend stocks for years, and the dividends usually increase with time.

Penny Stocks

What is a Penny Stock?

A penny stock refers to company shares that are trading at a price that is below $5. Unlike other stocks that are sold on the common stock exchange markets, trading of penny stocks is done through over-the-counter bulletin board (OTCBB). They may also use pink sheets which are electronic quotation systems.

Small companies usually issue most of the common penny stocks. These companies may have assets worth less than $4 million. The shares are speculative and can carry a higher risk than other forms of stock.

The standard definition of penny stocks is according to the Securities and Exchange Commission (SEC) which is also in charge of the regulation of penny stocks.

How Do Penny Stocks Work?

The trading of penny stocks is like any other stock on the market. They experience high swing in prices when trading. Nonetheless, they are not as liquid as other stocks due to their small volume. Combining the various factors that affect penny stocks, the risks associated with its purchase are much higher than with regular stocks.

The penny stocks market consists of many companies without any form of history. Information on the stocks is also limited due to the absence of major institutional investors to provide coverage. The lack of knowledge reduces the ability of an investor to make profitable trading decisions.

If by chance you come across information regarding a penny stock, the credibility of the information may be an issue. It is because there is no SEC filing obligation for a penny stock.

Due to the low liquidity of penny stocks, getting a buyer to purchase the stocks at a profitable price can be difficult. In most cases, investors usually sell at prices that are not very favorable. Penny stocks are also open to the "pump and dump" strategy which is an action by price manipulators.

Why is Penny Stock Still an Attractive Investment?

If you consider the risks involved, it is easy to wonder why many people still decide to invest in penny stocks. The fluctuation in price or volatility of the markets is the main reason why many investors even go for penny stocks.

One of the significant impacts of fluctuation is the opportunity for a stock to grow from $0.5 to $4 within a time frame of one week. When investors consider the possibility of such price change, the risks associated with penny stocks become more bearable.

An important aspect to discuss if you are going to make the most of penny stocks is identifying them before they increase in price.

How Do You Identify Profitable Penny Stocks Before a Price Increase?

An increase in the price of penny stocks can also

be referred to as rallying. Your aim as a penny stock investor is to make your purchase before the rallying of the stocks. The emergence of new companies daily is a simple fact you have to accept as a penny stock investor. It would help if you also understood that a lot of these new companies start trading publicly as soon as they emerge.

Performing research on these emerging companies requires skill and time that many investors are not willing to provide. Applying the skills and taking the time to conduct thorough research on emerging companies is how penny stock investors can find rare gems in the market.

Unlike the more successful companies that investors can easily select, choosing a new company that will perform well on the market is not as simple. A penny stock investor usually depends on their information sources and research to make the right choice.

Assessing a Company Offering Penny Stocks

To make your profits off penny stocks, it is essential that you evaluate the company offering the penny stocks very carefully. By accurately assessing the company, you can avoid falling victim to "pump and dump" strategies that prove to be very useful with shell companies.

You can start by assessing the business operations of the company. The type of business a company operates helps in determining how effective "pump and dump" strategies will be with the company. Companies that do not have any primary business operation are not a good option for penny stocks investments. The business operations of a company should be real and sustainable if you hope to make profits.

It would help if you also looked for the footnotes of the company. An important part of filing is the footnote. With larger companies, overlooking the notes may not have any severe implication. With penny stocks, ignoring the footnotes is a considerable risk. Reading the footnotes of a penny stock company can help you avoid things like non-GAAP accounting oddities.

The last area you need to assess is the financials of the penny stocks company. In addition to the financial statement quality, you should also be looking for the auditing firm of the company and how early filings are done in the company.

Selecting a Penny Stock Broker

Your success as a stock investor largely depends on your broker. With penny stocks, you should first consider the volume restrictions that the broker imposes. There are penny stock brokers that charge on substantial orders while there are others that do not charge a fee regardless of the order volume.

Another consideration is a limitation to your penny stocks trading amount. Some brokers may charge a commission after you trade an amount of penny stock shares in a day. This limitation can have a significant impact on your ability to trade profitably.

The trading options available to you also matter. There are penny stock brokers that offer online platforms with features that you will find with other forms f stock trades. You don't want to pick one that limits your trades to placing phone orders.

An Illustration to Show How Much You Can Earn With Penny Stocks

If you are a small-time investor or a beginner, it is possible you don't have enough money to invest in a substantial amount of Microsoft, Apple, or Facebook stocks. Instead, you decide to invest in more affordable stocks where your capital can go a long way.

If you have a capital of $5,000, then you can find a penny stock that is trading $1 stocks. You may decide to buy 5,000 shares of this penny stock. We are assuming the trade is successful (many investors lose on a deal, it is quite common) in this case.

As a result of rallying, the price of the penny stock shoots up from an abysmal $1 to $4 within two weeks. In this case, your investment increases to $20,000 which is a profit of $15,000; this is a sweet deal that is almost impossible to pass up.

Small-Cap Stocks

Stocks of a company that is publicly traded with a market capitalization that sits between the range of $300 million to $2 billion is referred to as a small cap stock. The total market value of the stocks of such a company is a determinant of its capitalization.

While the "cap" stands for capitalization, the "small" in a small cap stock represents the number of shares that are available for purchase. A common feature of small-cap stocks is the high price of the commodities.

For an individual investor, a small-cap stock is

more beneficial, and it is more difficult for institutional investors to buy small-cap stocks, this is due to the SEC filing requirements that a purchase of a large block of small-cap stocks the institutional investors will trigger.

It is easier for institutional investors to purchase large-cap stocks without triggering the filing requirement since the large block of shares that represents a high percentage of a small cap company is usually equivalent to a fraction of a large-cap company.

The disadvantage of the SEC filing is the rapid increase in stock prices as well as information on the purchase spreading to the public domain.

For an easy way to use the small cap stock in determining the capitalization of a company, consider a company with 40 million shares on the market. If these shares are available at $30 per share, then the total market capitalization is the result of the multiplication of the share price by the number of shares.

- Market capitalization = 40 million shares x $30 = $1.2 billion

The market capitalization is within the range of a small-cap stock.

Large-Cap Stocks

When the market capitalization of a company is over $10 billion, then its stocks fall within the range of large-cap stocks. A short for large market capitalization stocks, this is one of the three classifications of the stocks offered by companies on the market.

Some of the companies with the largest market capitalization include Microsoft, Apple, and Alphabet. The top benchmark indexes usually list large-cap companies. These indexes include Nasdaq Composite, S&P 500, and the Dow Jones Industrial Average.

There are certain features of large-cap stocks which make them a great investment option. These include:

Dividend-Paying Stocks

With a large cap stock, the payout ratio of the dividends is much higher than other types of shares. In addition to being higher, the profits are also stable and regular making them great for income distribution.

Transparency

The transparency of large-cap companies is noticeable in the amount of information available about these companies. The data makes it possible for investors to analyze the stocks and dividends payouts of the company correctly.

Impact on the Market

To become a large-cap company, the earnings of a company will have reached a level that is usually very stable. They serve as market leaders and news regarding a large company will often have a significant influence on the market.

Why Invest in Large Cap Stocks?

Diversification of a portfolio is the most

significant reason for investing in large-cap stocks. Investors also use large cap stocks in building up their investment portfolios since the stocks are often safer and provide higher returns.

When building a stock investment portfolio, combining small-cap, mid-cap, and large-cap stocks is always a good idea that yields sizable returns.

Marijuana Stocks

Marijuana stocks are steadily becoming more popular with lots of investors due to its legalization in several states in the United States. There are currently about 33 states where cannabis is legal in the U.S. while it is legalized at the federal level in countries like Canada. Although the industry is still in its early years, many companies possess billions in market capitalization within the industry.

If you want to understand how marijuana stock investments work concerning regular stocks, they are very similar. Regardless, there are a few differences that make marijuana stocks unique.

Depending on your investing strategy, there are various investment options for the marijuana industry. In addition to ETFs, it is also possible to invest in the cannabis industry through exchanges. There are some marijuana companies currently listed on the NYSE and NASDAQ which enables trading of their stocks.

Other companies that are unable to make it to the larger exchanges trade their stocks over-the-counter while smaller exchanges may also list the stocks of these companies. The downside to this trading option includes issues when trying to purchase the stocks as well as lower liquidity.

A prevalent method of investing in marijuana stocks is to buy pure-play cannabis stocks. These are stocks of cannabis growing companies. In terms of exposure, these companies offer the most on the markets.

Chapter 3: Investment Funds

What is an Investment Fund?

An investment fund involves a group of investors coming together to generate a large amount of capital for investments. The fund uses all the money in purchasing shares and then allocates shares to each investor based on the size of their investment. Each investor has complete control over their shares.

With an investment fund, individuals can gain access to investment opportunities that they cannot afford alone. The investment funds also reduce the cost of entry and offer better management of investments.

The assets the funds are used to acquire is not determined by any of the investors. Before pooling money into a fund, the investor can analyze the fee, risk, aim, and other factors that govern the investment fund. If the fund meets their requirements, investors can then choose the fund.

With the fund manager operating the fund, they have control over the purchase and sale of securities. Some funds focus on a single industry while others cover broad areas.

Investment funds include the popular mutual funds along with money market funds, hedge funds, and exchange-traded funds.

There are two main types of investment funds available. These are the open-end and closed-end investment funds.

Opportunities for Making Money Through Investment Funds

There are various opportunities available for making money through investment funds. Understanding the option that best suits you is very important.

Mutual Funds

A mutual fund is an investment that consists of money from various investors. These investors put their money into this fund in a bid to gain access to more profitable investment opportunities. These opportunities would have otherwise been impossible to achieve due to their high requirements.

The funds are used in the purchase of assets like bonds and stocks. These assets or securities do not belong to a single investor. Nonetheless, each investor with money in the mutual fund is eligible to an equal share of the returns from investment. They also bear the losses equally.

There are various reasons why many investors prefer to invest in mutual funds. One of these reasons is the opportunity to diversify their portfolio through a single investment. It also eliminates the need for continuous research and market analysis by the investor.

The diversification of the investments through a

mutual fund is the job of a fund manager. The fund manager is responsible for the management of mutual funds. Due to the active management of the funds by the fund manager, there are usually fees you would have to pay when investing in a mutual fund.

Mutual funds are also very attractive to investors who are still beginners. Since a fund manager is usually in charge of the investments, the investor does not need to have experience. The success of the mutual funds depends on the expertise of the fund manager.

Since the task of managing a mutual fund is the job of the fund manager, it means their job depends on the success of the funds. As an investor, you are providing a form of capital through which they can earn a tremendous amount of money if they do a great job. It is one of the reasons why mutual funds are often very dependable.

How Do I Make Money From Mutual Funds?

The main reason for investment is to make profits. So how do investors earn profits from the mutual funds?

There are three different ways through which you can get profits from this investment opportunity. These include:

Dividends

Since the mutual fund usually consists of various securities, there will be dividends on these securities. As soon as the profits from the securities are paid, an investor will receive an amount of the dividend that is equivalent to their investment. Depending on the investor, the dividends may either be reinvested or sent to an account.

Net Asset Value (NAV)

As an investment, there is an opportunity for the value of a mutual fund to increase. Due to the increase in value, the shares within the fund will also experience an increase in the purchase price. It is the NAV per share. As a result, if an investor decides to sell their investment, the rate will be much higher than the initial purchase value.

Capital Gain

Sale of securities is common with mutual funds. The sale of investments may result in either a profit or a loss. A capital gain arises from the sale of a security that has experienced an increase in price. If a security is sold after a fall in the price, it is a capital loss.

Mutual Fund Fees

Since the operation of the funds is usually in the hands of a fund manager, certain fees apply to the mutual funds. The more common charges can be separated into expense ratios and sales loads.

The Expense Ratio

The expense ratio refers to the expenses incurred during the operation of a mutual fund. These costs are usually deducted from the returns on the assets in the fund. These are costs which the investors pay for indirectly.

It is possible for investors to assess these costs under the "Annual Fund Operating Expenses" section in the prospectus of a mutual fund. Different fees usually make up these expenses, but it may vary depending on the mutual fund. They include the following:

Management Fee

It is also known as the hiring cost. The hiring cost is paid to the manager of the mutual fund. In most cases, it can be between 0.5% and 2% of the mutual fund assets. A high management fee does not imply that a mutual fund will perform better than those with a lower cost.

The management fee does not depend on the performance of the fund manager. It is a fee that must be paid regardless.

Account Fees

As an investor in a mutual fund, you may not have much money to invest in the fund. The result will be additional charges to operate your account. The funds usually have an amount that they set-up for these charges. If your account does not have a balance up to this amount, the charges will often apply.

Other Expenses

Certain expenses may not necessarily need a separate category. Such costs fall within this category. They include expenditures like accounting expenses, custodial expenses, record keeping, and other charges.

A distribution and service (12b-1) fee is also a part of the expense ratio. In general, the expense ratio on a mutual fund may be over 2% or as low as 0.25%.

Loads and Shareholder Fees

The loads on a mutual fund refer to the sales

commissions that the fund must pay. The compensation that the marketers and brokers receive fall within this category.

The shareholder fees cover the direct costs that a shareholder must pay due to buying and selling transactions of a mutual fund.

Sales Load

The sales load is easy to understand. It is the commission the broker receives. The commission may be paid as soon as you make a purchase or when you make a sale. There are two types of sales load which are the front-end loads and back-end loads.

The front-end load is a fee you pay the moment you purchase a fund. If you decide to invest the sum of $5,000 in a mutual fund that has a front-end load of 3%, the sales charge will be $150. Now, you have $4,850 that will be the investment in the fund.

The back-end load is not as simple as the front-end load. It is a sales charge that is collected after the sales of fund shares. It usually has a time-frame after which the payment will not apply.

In a simple example, consider a fund that requires the payment of a 4% back-end load that will reduce to 0% in the fifth year. Selling the fund in the first year will result in a 4% back-end load which reduces to 3%, 2%, 1%, and 0% in the second, third, fourth, and fifth year respectively. It implies that if you wait until the fifth year before selling, you will not have to incur the back-end load.

Due to the sales load, mutual funds may also be divided into load funds and no-load funds. While the load funds charge commissions, the no-load fund does not charge any sales commission. A lot of mutual funds may also combine both the front-end and back-end loads.

Purchase Fee

The purchase fee is a fee that the investor must pay to the fund for obtaining fund shares. It is not paid to the broker in this case and is therefore not a sales load.

Redemption Fee

It is a fee that a mutual fund may charge anytime an investor decides to sell their shares within the fund. According to SEC regulations, the redemption fee will not exceed 2%. It is separate from the back-end sales load on the funds.

Hedge Funds

A hedge fund is a form of investment partnership between investors and a fund manager. The investors are also known as limited partners. In most cases, the structure of the hedge fund is usually in the form of a limited liability company or a limited partnership.

It is like a mutual fund in the way it generates funds. In the hedge fund, the funds used in investments is made up of the money pooled together by the various investors in the fund. Unlike other investments like the mutual funds, the regulation of hedge funds by the Securities and Exchange Commission (SEC) is minimal.

A hedge fund is designed to incorporate a technique that is commonly known as hedging. It implies reducing the risk on the investments. There are also lots of additional investment techniques that hedge funds incorporate to earn high returns.

With most investments, higher risk means more returns on investments. In a hedge fund, the goal is to get the same high returns while significantly reducing the risks. It is a complicated task that makes hedge fund managers precious assets in the investment sector.

There are lots of techniques that a fund manager may utilize in achieving the maximum returns with the lowest possible risk. One of such methods is leveraging. Through leveraging, a hedge fund manager can borrow additional money to use in investing. Since there is more money to invest, the fund manager may decide to spend more money in low-risk investments to generate higher returns for the investors.

What Do Hedge Funds Invest in?

The hedge fund manager is fully responsible for the investment strategy they implement. Nonetheless, the plan must be following what they initially communicated to investors.

Various hedge funds specialize in different areas of investments. Several hedge funds focus on real estate investments while there are others that efficiently trade junk bonds. You can also find hedge funds that will concentrate on buying stocks and avoid selling short.

Is it an Investment Opportunity Accessible to Everyone?

There are government regulations that are in place to determine those that are eligible for investing in hedge funds. Those that qualify for investments are known as "accredited investors."

There are times when a fund manager may decide to make an exception in admitting an investor. It is legal for hedge funds to admit up to 35 investors that are not accredited. Gaining a slot through this method may be very difficult.

The conditions that an investor must meet to be accredited are stated below. The investor only needs to meet one of these conditions to qualify as an accredited investor:

- An annual personal income that is equal to $200,000 or more for two consecutive years with proof that they will be able to maintain this income level. As a couple, the requirement remains the same with the only difference being a minimum combined income of $300,000 per annum.

- Should be a director, partner, executive, or any other individual that has a relationship with the hedge fund.

- Without the primary residence, the personal net worth of the investor should be at least $1 million. The personal net worth may be as an individual or as a couple.

The conditions listed above are just some of those available. In addition to joining the hedge fund as an accredited investor, some also participate as "sophisticated investors." Anyone that has the experience and is knowledgeable in assessing the benefits and risks associated with the investment is a sophisticated investor.

What is Two and Twenty in Hedge Funds?

The "2 and 20" refers to the most common compensation scheme utilized by hedge fund managers. According to this scheme, the fund manager is entitled to annual compensation of 2% of the assets and 20% of the profits as compensation.

That said, this is perhaps the most challenging thing for investors to accept when putting their money into a hedge fund. It implies that your fund manager may get as much as $4 million on a $200 million fund without turning in any profits. Either profit or loss, the manager receives the compensation.

A "high water mark' feature is becoming common in hedge funds. Through this feature, fund managers are required to turn in profits on a fund that has previously lost some of its investments. Without bringing in a reasonable amount of gain, the manager will not be entitled to the additional compensations.

Hedge Fund Regulation

The minimal regulation which hedge funds enjoy form the SEC makes it different from other investment opportunities. Since the funds are received from only accredited investors, there is a general belief that these individuals can assess the risk that comes with the investment opportunity.

Remember, there is minimal regulation. It means that the fund is regulated to a certain degree.

Following the SEC regulations, a higher number of investors in a hedge fund need to have accreditation.

In recent years, hedge funds are beginning to gain more attention from regulatory bodies. There is also the hedge fund advertising aspect of this investment. The use of internet, print, and television in promoting the investment products of the fund to accredited investors is known as hedge fund advertising.

Before a fund can start an advertising campaign, it needs to fill out a Form D and submit it to the SEC. The submission of the form must be at least 15 days beforehand.

How Do You Profit From Hedge Funds?

To invest in a hedge fund, it is best that you have a reasonable amount of money to invest. Many hedge funds will require at least $1 million to invest.

The first step in joining a hedge fund is to find a

suitable hedge fund on the market. There are several hedge funds on the market, and prominent individuals run some. They are usually a limited liability company (LLC).

Once you find a possible hedge fund, you should receive an operating agreement that you need to read. The operating agreement is a form of legal document that accurately explains how the hedge fund operates.

In this case, let us assume the operating condition states that the hedge fund manager will receive 20% of profits over 4% per year. The document may also indicate that the hedge fund manager can invest the money using any investment instrument available to them.

Now, it is your turn to play your part. As an investor, you decide to invest $50 million along with four other investors. It would mean a total of $250 million in investments. The hedge fund puts the money from investors into a brokerage account and begins investing according to the conditions in the operating agreement.

The goal of the hedge fund manager is to ensure that they are getting the highest returns possible while minimizing the risk on the investments. It is the job they must do daily. Their profits depend on how much they can increase the yields.

After all the investments, a year goes by and the hedge fund increases by 40%. Now, the hedge fund is worth $350 million. According to the operating agreement, the investors receive the first 4% of the profits which amounts to $4 million.

4% is the hurdle rate on investment. As the name implies, it is a form of a hurdle for the hedge fund manager to cross. Without getting over this hurdle rate, the manager is not entitled to any additional performance compensation. In this case, they get additional compensation since the hedge fund is over the hurdle rate.

After deducting the 4%, the capital gain on the

hedge fund becomes $96 million. It is split 20% and 80% to manager and investors respectively. The investors will receive $76.8 million with each investor earning a share of $15,360,000.

It means that you will get a total of $15.36 million on your $50 million investment.

Money Market Funds

What is a Money Market Fund?

A money market fund invests only in money market securities. Money market securities refer to cash and securities that are cash equivalent. Money market funds are usually short-term investment opportunities that are very liquid.

Instruments that money market funds usually invest in include:

- Bankers' Acceptances

- Certificates of deposit (CDs)

- Repurchase agreements

- U.S. Treasuries

- Commercial paper

In the way it operates, there are some similarities between a money market fund and a mutual fund. Like the mutual funds, it performs based on SEC regulations and investors also receive shares from the fund.

The weighted average maturity (WAM) of a money market fund portfolio must be less than or equal to sixty days. Furthermore, this is according to the rules of the Securities and Exchange Commission (SEC).

Features of a Money Market Funds

There are certain features of money market funds that make it a unique investment. These include:

Little Initial Investment

Many investors find it difficult to purchase most money market securities individually due to the high requirements for purchase. With a money market fund, investors can invest a minimal amount of money along with other investors to gain access to these securities.

Safety

Most money market securities are investments that are usually safe. The returns on the securities remain profitable while also reducing the default risk through the purchase of debt securities. Government, banks, and large corporations are usually the issuers of these securities. There is also a short maturity on the securities.

Ease of Access

The problem with a few investments is the inability to access the funds until a specific time. With money market funds, the shares are very easy to access in case an investor decides to buy or sell. To achieve ease of access, investors can write checks and receive payments on the same day.

Understanding the Two Categories of Money Market Funds

If you decide to invest in a money market fund, it is crucial that you know the groups of money market funds available. The two categories are the taxable and tax-free money market funds.

As the name implies, taxable money market funds are those on which you may have to pay regular federal and state taxes on the investment returns. There are lots of investments that may be taxable money market funds, and they include investments in CDs, bankers' acceptances, repurchase agreement, government agency securities, and commercial paper.

The tax-free money market funds are exempted from tax payments to a reasonable extent. This exemption limits the investment options that are available to this category of money market funds. In most cases, they often have a low return on investment.

Deciding Between a Tax-Free and Taxable Money Market Fund

Although taxable money market funds offer a higher yield than the tax-free funds, it is possible for investors to lose additional returns after taxes. To ensure you are choosing the right option, it is essential that you compare the yield on both funds.

To achieve an accurate comparison, it is crucial that you deduce the equivalent taxable yield from a tax-free return.

To calculate the equivalent taxable yield, the following equation applies:

- Equivalent taxable yield = tax-free yield ÷ (1 − marginal tax rate)

A quick example to show the application of this formula, consider an individual that falls within the 22% tax bracket. You may find an excellent taxable money market fund that offers a yield of 1.6%. Since you need to compare with a tax-free money market fund, suppose you see one with a 1.4% yield. The formula will apply.

Inputting the values into the formula will give:

- Equivalent taxable yield = (0.014 ÷ [1-0.22])

- Equivalent taxable yield = 0.0179 or 1.79%

From the calculation, the equivalent taxable yield is higher than the yield on the taxable money market fund. It will be a better option to go for the tax-free yield in this case.

Exchange-Traded Funds

An Exchange-Traded fund is a liquid financial instrument that is used in tracking commodities, bonds, stocks, and other assets. As an investment fund, ETF shares trade like stocks on the exchange market. It is a feature that differentiates it from mutual funds.

Due to buying and selling of the ETF shares, the prices move in either an up or down direction during the trading times. Many investors prefer to invest in ETFs rather than in mutual funds since ETFs offer reduced fees and an increased daily volume.

Investors can decide to use hedging, income, or speculation strategies in trading ETFs on the market. The asset determines the price of the ETF it is tracking. It can be gold bullion, shares, or oil futures. Through ownership of these assets, it is possible to split the ownership into shares that can be distributed among investors.

A Unit Investment Trust (UIT) is a type of ETF that should have a set date on which the fund must come to an end. Regardless, the ETF still has the option of extending this date making it operate like an open-ended fund.

Dividends and interests on investments which the ETF earns must be distributed among the investors in the fund. ETFs also reduce tax costs through shares listing on an exchange. There is no need to redeem the shares when an investor wishes to buy or sell. The investor can merely go to the exchange for this purpose. Tax liability is often triggered by redeeming shares.

Another benefit of ETFs is the low average expense ratio that shareholders get to enjoy. The expense ratio will vary depending on the underlying asset of the ETF.

If you buy ETF shares worth $20,000 at $16 for each share and then there is a 25% increase in price within five weeks. It means the new price will be $20. Your ETFs will now be worth $25,000 which means a profit of $5,000.

Chapter 4: Real Estate

What is Real Estate?

Any land-based property you own is a real estate. In addition to the land, it also includes natural resources and the structures on the land.

What is Real Estate Investing?

Making money through the sale, purchase, lease, or ownership of structures and the land beneath these structures is real estate investing. There are three classifications of real estate investing. They include the following:

Residential Real Estate

Buildings that serve as living spaces to individuals are referred to as residential real estate. It can be a condominium, townhouse, single-family home, and multi-family home.

If a home exceeds four units, then it automatically becomes a commercial property.

Townhouses and freestanding homes fall within this category.

Industrial Real Estate

Power plants, factories, and storage warehouse are also a part of real estate. In the case of these properties, they are useful for industrial businesses.

Commercial Real Estate

Properties that are designed and used for business purposes are referred to as commercial real estate. There are four sub-classifications of commercial real estate, and they include multi-family, land, office, and retail. A large apartment building is a multi-family, farmland is a land, a business office building is an office, while restaurants serve as retail.

How Can You Earn Money as a Real Estate Investor?

The main reason for investing your money in real estate is usually to gain profits. As a real estate investor, there are three means through which you can make profits on your investments. These include the following:

Appreciation

The appreciation of a property is one of the significant sources of profit in a real estate investment. The possible profit that an investor can gain through the sale of a property is the appreciation on the property. The property serves as the equity that the investor sells for profit.

The sale of an investment property usually provides a single, massive return. It is what differentiates appreciation from rent and loans.

Rent

The income you earn through the lease of a property is the rent on the property. Rather than providing a single, massive return, it can serve as a source of a monthly stream of income. It is like a loan in this regard.

The management of a rental property may be in

the hands of the investor or a property management company. Furthermore, this depends on if the investor is using an active or passive investment style. There will be a need to split the rent between both parties in a case where a property management company is involved.

Loans

This is a real estate loan or a debt investment. In this situation, a property owner or real estate developer receives a credit from the investor. The repayment of the interest on the loan serves as a steady income stream to the investor.

A debt can be unsecured or secured, a mezzanine debt, a junior debt, or a senior debt. These differences arise due to the number of lenders. Debt investment is a tool that real estate investment platforms, private equity firms, and REITs use as a form of passive investment.

Benefits of Real Estate Investment

There are various benefits of real estate investments which make them suitable for beginner investors. Below are some of the reasons why you should consider real estate investments when beginning your career as an investor.

- It is a tangible investment opportunity for investors. It is easy to see, touch, and show off a real estate investment to anyone that cares to know.

- During periods of inflation, having a real estate investment can be excellent protection against a decrease in the purchasing power of the currency of a country.

- For most investors, they have much knowledge regarding real estate investments opportunities. Many individuals usually have easy access to information regarding real estate from a very early age.

- The option of inspecting a property before investing makes it possible to avoid falling victim of a fraud. Since you can assess the property, you will be sure to get what you pay for.

- Debt investments (leverage) in real estate investments are safer than using leverage in trading stocks.

How to Invest in Real Estate

Invest in a Company That Offers Real Estate Services

Companies providing real estate services generally do not buy real estate properties. Such companies include commercial real estate developers, hotels, timeshare companies, resort operators, and those that may engage in the sales of homes through an agent in the industry.

In terms of operation, they do not operate like real estate REITs. If you want to invest in such companies, there are a lot of them available. The issue is the difficulty in finding profitable companies in this sector. A lot of them usually pay a lower dividend to investors than what REITs offer.

If you are looking for a great way to diversify your investment portfolio, then you shouldn't overlook this option.

Real Estate Exchange-Traded Funds (ETFs)

If you decide to get into real estate investments, then similar to other industries, real estate ETFs are also available. The securities that real estate ETF invests in differ from one to the other. Certain ETFs choose to invest in REITs stocks. This form of investment offers a lower risk than a direct investment in the REITs.

A popular real estate ETF is IYR while another is the Vanguard Real Estate ETF or VNQ. The VNQ is an ETF that invests in the stocks of popular real estate investment funds.

Buying Vacation Property

Vacation property is usually a property you purchase in an area where people enjoy taking holidays. In such areas, you can expect to receive tenants looking for a place to stay during their short visit.

Due to the location of the property, it can be a very profitable venture. Nonetheless, it can also have a very high cost of purchase and maintenance.

To purchase a vacation property, you may need as much as $400,000. Your earning on this vacation property can average $50,000 per annum. Your yearly income may also be higher when you consider appreciation.

Flipping Houses

It is a prevalent form of real estate investing. As an investor, in this case, you buy a home that needs renovation and then put in a good deal of money to renovate the house. The improvement will help increase the market value of the property to ensure it brings in a profitable price on the market.

As an investment option, it requires many funds. The funds include the initial cost of purchase, cost of renovations, and cost of owning the home. In an ideal situation, the investor will only hold the house for a brief time. When the home remains in possession of the investor for long periods, it can result in a loss.

Some of the renovations that you will be performing include a change in the plans, replacing the floorings, and changing the countertops. Making these improvements to match the current market requirements usually yield positive results.

Depending on the house and the location, flipping houses can generate a substantial amount of income. Flipping houses in specific areas can earn you an average gross profit of about $45,000 per flip. In some cases, this value can be a lot higher.

Invest by Buying Commercial, Non-Residential Properties

Before you think of jumping into this investment opportunity, it is crucial that you understand that it costs a lot more than residential property investments. For this reason, it is beneficial to partner with other investors in this case. Commercial property includes any building that is used for business purposes such as office buildings, warehouses, retail stores, garage, shopping malls, and more.

In contrast to residential properties, the lease contracts on commercial buildings are usually longer. Also, profits are also very high. It is one of the real estate investment options that offers a high-risk, high-reward.

The profits on a commercial property investment usually depend on the cap rate. A lower cap rate improves the value of your commercial property. With a commercial property worth $300,000 and a cap rate of 7%, you can generate about

$21,000 in annual income. The leasing party bears the maintenance costs on commercial properties according to the lease in most cases.

Invest in Companies That Offer Home Construction Services

Home construction is a service sector that will continue to grow. People will always require a new home, and there will also be renovations of existing homes. These are the reasons why these companies keep experiencing growth.

If you believe that home construction will continue to increase, then investing in real estate construction is a suitable investment opportunity. There are lots of companies that focus on home constructions. There are large construction companies that are also publicly traded on the stock exchange market.

A few construction companies that you can assess for investment opportunities include Pulte Homes (PMH), D.R. Horton (DHI), LGI Homes (LGIH), and Lennar (LEN). These are some of the major construction companies, but there are lots of others you can also consider.

Wholesaling Houses

When you decide to go into wholesaling of real estate, you work as a middleman. In this form of investment, you as the wholesaler will be entering into a contract with a seller. You then look for a buyer who is willing to pay a higher amount for the property.

The difference between the amount you receive and the amount on the contract is your profit as the wholesaler. Many people consider wholesaling to be like flipping houses. There are a few differences that make wholesaling less risky and sometimes more profitable.

In wholesaling, you don't need to own the home, pay maintenance fees, or pay for the cost of owning the home. You can also adjust the buying contract to ensure that you can pull out in a case where finding a buyer becomes an issue.

Understanding how you can make profits from wholesaling houses is quite simple. Consider a situation where you find a home that is underpriced at $50,000 but requires repairs which estimate at $30,000. If you determine that the house will be worth $110,000 after repairs, it is now time to find a buyer.

If you are lucky to get a buyer that is willing to pay $70,000 for the house, then you will be able to make $20,000 in profit after paying the original seller, this is without ever owning the home.

Real Estate Investment Trust (REITs)

A Real Estate Investment Trust, REIT, refers to companies that possess real estate properties such as retail spaces, hotels, office buildings, and apartments. A large portion of the income such companies generate come from investments in the real estate sector.

One of the benefits of REITs to investors is the opportunity to invest in real estate without owning any actual property. In addition to offering a high dividend, these companies provide a large percentage of the profit in dividends. Investors can choose to reinvest the dividends or use it as a source of regular income.

Several REITs do not trade publicly while others are available on the exchanges. The problem with a REIT that is not publicly traded is the difficulty of selling them.

Real Estate Mutual Funds

Just like regular mutual funds, this investment opportunity involves multiple investors putting their money together to form a large pool with the primary purpose of investing.

With an investment manager operating the fund, through this investment opportunity, investors can gain access to various real estate securities.

Depending on the preference of an investor, the mutual fund may invest in either income-oriented investments or growth-oriented investments. The fund manager also ensures diversification of investments to minimize the risks to the investor.

Purchase Rental Property

A rental property is usually a long-term investment option. It includes industrial, commercial, and residential property. One of the benefits of a rental property is the availability of monthly cash flow in the form of rent.

Various factors determine the profitability of a rental property. The first is your ability to attract tenants to the property. To successfully get tenants to notice your property, you need to offer low rent. By minimizing your running expenses, you will be able to provide affordable rent.

You also have to decide on how to operate the property. You may need to delegate a few tasks to other individuals for effectiveness.

Being a great landlord is also essential. You need to ensure that the property remains in good condition and your tenants can reach you when it is necessary. If you are interested in turning the rental property into a passive investment, then a property management company can be helpful.

There is a one percent rule that most rental property investors follow when investing. According to this rule, any rental property you buy should be able to generate a minimum of 1% gross monthly rent. Following this simple rule, a $300,000 rental property should be able to create a minimum of $3,000 in rent. You can analyze this using the rate of return or cap rate of the property. Your annual earning on this property will be $36,000 before any deduction.

An excellent rate of return is between the range of 10% - 12%.

Chapter 5: Forex

The Forex Markets

Foreign Exchange, currency trading, or FX are different terms used in describing the foreign exchange market. With over $5 trillion of daily average trading volume, the forex market remains the world's largest market with high liquidity. If you don't understand the implication of this, put simply, the trading volume of the forex market is more than the combination of all stock exchanges.

Trading on the Forex Market

Many individuals perform forex transactions every day without any knowledge of what they are doing. It is as simple as exchanging your U.S. dollars for Euro any time you take a trip from the United States to Italy. In this process, there are two currencies and an exchange rate, the necessary factors for a forex transaction.

Trading on the forex market is in a bid to earn money by correctly predicting the price movement of a currency against another currency. If you want to travel to Paris from New York and you convert 1,000 dollars to Euros, you may get €900. After your vacation, you have exactly half of what you left with which is now €450. Following the previous rate of exchange, this amount should be equivalent to $500. If there have been some substantial economic events before your return, you may find out that the money you want to exchange is now worth $600, a profit of about $100.

In the above description, trading on the forex market involves looking to make profits from the small price movements. If the example above was an actual trade, it means that the gains on the trade amount to $100.

Types of Forex Trading

Scalping

It is a forex trading style in which a forex trader

holds a position for a short time. It can be as short as a few seconds or sometimes up to a few minutes. It is a fast-paced form of forex trading.

In this form of trading, the trader will have to watch the charts for most of the day. Their primary goal is to get little amounts of pips as many times as possible on different trades. Furthermore, adding up the little pips from different trades will yield a reasonable profit.

This form of trading is best for individuals that are not after massive wins. It is suitable for individuals that are comfortable making small gains over a long period. Quick thinking and undivided attention are necessary for success in scalping.

If you decide to become a scalper, then it is essential you perform your trading during the busiest times which is when there are overlapping market sessions. It would help if you also traded the very liquid pairs such as GDP/USD, USD/JPY, and EUR/USD.

Day Trading

Day trading is like scalping, but it also has its unique features. Like scalping, it is a trading style that is short term. Unlike scalping, the trader is only opening a single position that will be closed at the end of the trading day.

One of the essential features of day trading is that the trades never extend overnight. It is a form of trading that is suitable for traders that will be able to monitor the trade all through the day.

There are three main types of day trading. They include the following:

- Trend trading

- Countertrend trading

- Breakout trading

Trend trading is a form of day trading in which a trader determines the overall trend direction using a longer time frame. Once the trader establishes the course, they can then decide on the best entry point in the direction of the trend using a shorter time frame.

In countertrend trading, a trader will also determine the overall trend using a longer time frame and then move to a shorter time frame. On the shorter time frame, the trader will look for trading opportunities in the opposite direction of the trend.

In forex, a currency pair may sometimes form support and resistance. These are highs and lows on the chart which the price of the currency pair does not exceed. In breakout trading, a trader is banking on the chances that the cost will soon exceed either one of these prices.

Swing Trading

When a forex trader decides to hold a trade position for days, it is known as swing trading. If you are an individual that only gets a few hours free to monitor the charts in a day, then swing trading is a good option.

This long-term trading style is suitable for traders that have a job or those attending lectures. With this style, traders can monitor and analyze market trends for a few hours in a day.

Since they will hold the trade position for a more extended period, the stop losses are more substantial. The trade will be open to massive price fluctuations, and it is vital that the trader does not give in to emotions during these periods. Therefore, a good trading strategy is essential.

Position Trading

Position trading is a very long-term trading style that is not suitable for many traders. It is a trading position that can be open for months and even years. It requires much patience on the part of the trader to be able to hold such trades.

In position trading, fundamental analysis is preferable. The primary study is more suitable for analyzing the behavior of currency pairs concerning the economic data of a country.

If you will let your emotions get the best of you, then position trading is not the right style for you. There are bound to be situations when the market prices will be against your trade. These market movements can be massive which is why large stop losses are necessary for position trading.

Learning With a Demo Account

Since forex trading is a form of investment in which you can lose all your money in a short time, practice is critical. When you visit the site of a forex broker, a lot of them offer what is known as a "demo account."

The demo account is a free account that provides virtual money for free trading without profits on the forex market. The demo account has all the features of a real account with the only exception being the use of virtual money to trade.

You can consider the demo account as a trial period with a broker. It allows you to understand how their platform works and the features they offer. During the trading period, you are protected from the risks that come with a real trading account.

With a demo account, you can test new forex trading strategies, assess your skills, and fully understand how forex trading works. The best part of the account is trading without any risk.

If you want to make the most of forex trading, then you must use a demo trading account. The account will be beneficial in developing a unique trading system that is profitable. You can achieve this system before you decide to fund a trading account with real money.

To properly utilize a demo forex trading account, you must be patient. Through patience, you can overcome the temptation of opening a live trading account. Being patient and waiting until your strategy starts yielding positive results on a demo account, then you will be successful on a live trading account.

Consistency is critical with a trading system. You need to run a trading account for at least three months to determine if your trading strategy can successfully offer favorable outcomes.

As a beginner in forex trading, it is essential you choose a currency pair you will be trading. It is easier to monitor a single currency and develop a trading strategy when you are just getting into forex trading.

Choosing a primary currency is beneficial since the spreads are usually tighter and they have higher liquidity becoming a successful trader will require practice, dedication, good judgment, patience, and hard work. A demo trading account can help you hone these skills.

Making Money From Forex Trading

Making money through forex trading depends on buying and selling of currencies on the forex market. People who have experience trading on the stock market will find it very easy to learn forex trading.

As a trader in the forex market, you are exchanging currencies while anticipating a price change.

To fully understand how to make money forex trading, there are various aspects of forex trading you need to understand. These include the following:

Forex Quotes

When trading forex, quoting of the currencies is done in pairs. The pairing of currencies is because forex trading involves the purchase of one currency and the sale of another simultaneously.

Common currency quotes in the forex market include the GBP/USD, USD/CHF, EUR/USD, and AUD/USD.

In a forex quote, the first currency is the base currency. It is the currency that appears on the left side of the forward slash ("/"). The currency on the right side is the quote currency.

In the EUR/USD currency pair, the base currency is the EUR (European Euro) while the quote currency is the USD (U.S. dollar).

The currency quote is essential in determining the exchange rate of a currency on the forex market. The price is also dependent on if you are buying or selling.

If you decide to buy a currency pair, the forex quote is an indication of the cost of one unit of the base currency in terms of the quote currency. If you decide to sell a currency pair, the forex quote indicates the units of the quote currency you can get any time you choose to sell a unit of the base currency.

Buying or Selling a Currency Pair

In forex trading, you must decide on the right time to buy a currency pair or sell a currency pair; this is how you earn money from trading. When you determine that the price of the base currency will increase in value in comparison to the quote currency, then you will buy a currency pair.

On the other hand, if you determine that the value of the base currency will lose value in comparison to the quote currency, then you will sell the currency.

What Do Long or Short Mean in Forex Trading?

The terms long and short in forex trading are just the traders' terms for buy and sell. When you decide to buy a currency pair, you are going long. If you choose to sell a currency pair, you are going short.

What is the Bid, Ask, and Spread in Forex?

When you find a forex quote on the market, you will usually see two prices on a quote. The two prices consist of the bid and ask prices. These prices are essential to any trader entering or exiting a trade.

The bid price is essential when going short while the asking price is critical when going long.

Bid Price

The bid price is the price at which you will be able to sell a base currency. It is the price at which the market is willing to buy a currency pair from the trader.

As an example, consider a EUR/USD currency pair. If you have a quote as EUR/USD 1.2412/17, then 1.2412 represents the bid price. It is usually the price that appears on the left side of the forward slash.

In the example above, you can sell one European Euro for the price of 1.2412 U.S. dollars.

Ask Price

The asking price of a currency pair is also known as the offer price. It is the price at which you will be able to buy a single unit of the base currency. It is merely the price at which the market is willing to sell a currency to a trader.

Using the previous example, we have the quote as EUR/USD 1.2412/17. In this case, you can purchase one Euro for the price of 1.2417 U.S. dollars.

Spread

A spread is a value you obtain when you calculate the difference between the bid price and the asking price. Using the currency quote, EUR/USD 1.2412/17, we can determine the spread. This quote can be written as EUR/USD = 1.2412/1.2417 in full.

The difference between the bid and ask price above is 0.0005 which is equivalent to 5 pips.

What is a Pip in Forex Trading?

In a price quote, the smallest value of a price change is a pip. It is the last decimal value. It depends on how the price quote appears.

In the common price quotes like the EUR/USD, 0.0001 will be equivalent to a pip. If there is a price change from 1.3452 to 1.3455, there is a price change of 0.0003 in the quote. This change is equivalent to 3 pips.

In other quotes such as the USD/JPY, 0.01 is equivalent to one pip. It is because most Japanese Yen pairs usually have two decimal places. If there is a change in price from 1.21 to 1.23 which is equal to 0.02, this is equal to two pips.

On various forex trading platforms, it is now common to find currency pairs quotes in 5 decimal places for the common pairs and three decimal places for those including the Japanese Yen.

This new form of quote involves the inclusion of a "pipette" in the quote.

What is a Pipette?

A pipette is available in quotes to five decimal places and two decimal places. A pipette may also be referred to as a fractional pip.

In a EUR/USD quote to five decimal places, a

change from 1.24573 to 1.24576 implies a 0.00003 change in the USD. The 0.00003 difference is equivalent to 3 pipettes.

The pipette on the trading platform will appear as a smaller digit on the right side of the two more significant figures in the quote.

Using Leverage in Forex Trading

Leverage in forex trading is what makes it possible to trade vast amounts as a small-time investor. It gives you the opportunity to use a small capital to gain control of a large sum of money for trading.

It is a form of borrowed capital you can use in gaining a higher return on your trade. The ratio of the transaction capital to the margin requirement is also the leverage.

Depending on the broker you are trading with, the leverage available will differ. When discussing leverage, consider it as an amount your broker is willing to borrow you for a deposit you are putting down. This deposit is what forex traders refer to as a margin.

The margin requirements will differ depending on the lot or position. The broker will deduct this amount from your account before you can trade. It is a deposit that the broker uses to prevent your balance from falling to a negative value.

Base Currency

In a currency pair, the base currency is the first currency in the pair. The quote of a currency pair is merely a comparison of how much the base currency is worth in terms of the quote currency.

In most cases, the base currency in the forex market is the U.S. dollars. This rule doesn't apply to the Euro, New Zealand dollar, British pound, and Australian dollar.

If you have a currency quote of USD/CAD = 1.5542, then it implies that one USD is worth 1.5542 CAD on the market.

Quote Currency

The second currency in the quote of a currency pair is the quote currency. In a currency pair, the forex quote indicates the amount of the quote currency you will need to be able to purchase one unit of the base currency.

Cross Currency

If you decide to trade a currency pair that does not include the U.S. dollar, then the pair is a cross currency. In a regular forex pair, the price behavior of a cross currency will differ from a pair that includes the U.S. dollar.

The primary benefit of a cross currency pair is the opportunity to bypass the conversion to the U.S. dollar and then converting it to the actual currency you need. Some of the standard cross currency pairs available include EUR/GBP. EUR/CHF, and GBP/JPY.

Major and Minor Currencies

In forex, certain currencies are more commonly

traded than the others. These currencies are the major currencies. They are referred to as 'majors' and have high liquidity. They include the EUR, USD, GBP, JPY, AUD, CHF, NZD, and CHF.

Any currency that is not a part of these eight major currencies is a minor currency in forex trading.

Lot

A lot refers to the total units of a currency a forex trader will buy or sell. Lot sizes are available in a Nano, micro, mini, and standard size which are equal to 100 units, 1,000 units, 10,000 units, and 100,000 units of currency.

To make a reasonable amount of profits or loss on a forex trade, the amount of currency units needs to be reasonably large. It is to complement pip gain on a trade.

For a simple look at how the lot size and pip value work together to produce a significant change, consider a trade that includes the

USD/CAD currency pairs. If you open a mini lot size that is equal to 10,000 currency units, look below to see how it affects your trade.

- USD/CAD trading at an exchange rate of 1.3472 = (0.0001/1.3472) x 10,000 = $0.74 per pip

The above calculation is only valid for currency pairs where the USD is the base currency.

Margin

The margin on an account is the minimum deposit that your forex broker requires. The minimum deposit will vary depending on the forex broker you are trading with. It is an amount that the forex broker will keep as a deposit anytime you decide to open a trade.

Calculating Your Profits (or Loss) on a Trade

We have established the importance of leverage and pip value on the profits and loss on a trade.

Now, how do you use this in calculating the profits on a specific trade?

In this case, let us assume you decide to buy U.S. dollars (USD) and sell Canadian dollars. If the rate for this currency pair is quoted as 1.3472/1.3479, then you will buy at 1.3479 which is the asking price of the currency pair.

You may decide to use the leverage option to purchase a standard lot at the asking price of 1.3479 and then sell it the moment there is an increase in rate. If the price increases and the new price quote of the currency pair are 1.3509 / 1.3514, you can choose the sell option to close the trade. To sell, you will use the bid price of 1.3509 that is the acceptable buying price.

Calculating the difference between the previous ask price of 1.3479 and the current bid price of 1.3509, you have 30 pips. You can now calculate your profits using the previous formula.

The profit on the trade = (0.0001 /1.3509) x 100,000 = $7.4 per pip.

With 30 pips, your trade profit will be equal to $222

An Example to Show How Much You Can Make From a Forex Trade

In this case, let us assume that you are a day trader. To be a successful day trader, you must have a trading strategy with a high win rate. Your plan may not be perfect, but a strategy that wins on 60 percent of your daily trades is a great strategy.

If you have $10,000 as your trading capital, then you must ensure that you are not risking more than 1 percent on every trade, this is equal to $100 in this case. So, your stop-loss order should limit your trade losses to $100 on any trade. You can set a stop-loss order six pips below the entry price and ten pips above the entry price.

As a result, you will always earn more than you will lose. It is an essential feature of the strategy. You still want your wins to be able to cover your potential losses.

As a day trader, you may decide to perform 100 trades in a month. According to your trading strategy, you can achieve your 60 profitable trades for the month. If the pip value on the trade is $8.5, then a profit from any trade will be equal to $85. Since your stop-loss is set at six pips below entry price, then each loss on trade is worth $51.

Since you had 60 profitable trades, then you will earn a total of $5,100 for the month. Your losses will be equal to $2,040. The gross profit for the month will be similar to $3,060.

The gross profit is as a result of using estimates in our calculations. Your earnings may sometime be lower or higher. It all depends on your investment strategy and capital. Commissions charged by a broker may also lead to a reduction in your profits.

Chapter 6: Banking

What is a Bank?

A bank is a financial institution that receives deposits from investors for safe-keeping. They also provide loans to individuals through which they make profits. The profit of a bank is equal to the difference between the interest the bank charges and the interest paid by the bank.

The bank uses the deposits from account holders as capital for giving out loans to individuals and other corporate bodies. Money in a bank is like a pool of funds from different account holders which the bank uses to generate its profits.

What Establishments Qualify as a Financial Institution?

All establishments that perform deposit, investments and loan transactions are referred to as financial institutions. The role of each establishment within the financial institution differs. The financial institution consists of the following establishments:

- Commercial banks

- Insurance companies

- Investment banks

- Brokerages

- Investment companies

Other financial institutions do not qualify as banks but render similar services to customers. These include the following:

- Shadow banking systems

- Savings and loan associations

- Credit unions

Benefits of Investing in a Bank

There are two significant benefits of investing in a bank. These are the main reasons why people opt for bank investments regardless of the low returns they often get. Below are the two significant benefits:

Certainty

The high accuracy with which you can determine how much you will have at a specific date is one of the benefits of a bank investment. Unlike other investments, there is a fixed interest rate on bank investments, and it is not affected by fluctuations in market prices.

Certainty makes it a beneficial form of investment when you need to keep your capital for use in an emergency or when you need to gather an amount before a specific date to buy a house or a car.

Insurance

The safety of your investment is what makes bank investments very appealing. In this case, the investment is the money you decide to keep in the bank. Insurance is usually available with banks that have insurance coverage from the Federal Deposit Insurance Corporation (FDIC).

For each account holder, the insurance covers an account of up to $250,000. If the bank experiences any issue that causes it to shut down operations, you can be sure to receive all your money up to the $250,000 limit.

The insurance covers several accounts including CDs and savings account. As a bank customer, you may have $100,000 in CDs and another $100,000 in a savings account. In case the bank shuts down, you will get back both the money in the savings account and the CD since the total falls below the limit.

Opportunities for Investing in a Bank

High Yield Savings Account

One of the easiest ways to invest money is usually a savings account. They often have an interest rate that generally appeals to customers. If you want to gain a proper handle on your finances, a savings account can be helpful.

A common mistake most individuals make when

opening a savings account is to opt for a regular savings account. What many people fail to understand is that the interest rate will not hold up against the operational fees as well as inflation. As a result, it is possible to end up with an amount that is lower than your initial savings in the future.

If you want access to a more favorable interest rate, then a high-yield savings account is your best bet. This account type also offers the same reliability and security that is available on the regular savings account.

To enjoy the benefits of a high-yield savings account, you will need to do your research. The research is your way of determining the bank that offers the best Annual Percentage Yield (APY) on your savings.

Searching for a new bank may be difficult if your current bank seems to provide a high-yield account with a good APY. There are other factors you need to consider for the best profits from the account. Below are some of the things you need to think if you decide to compare accounts from various banks:

Minimum Initial Deposit

What is the minimum amount you need to have if you choose to open the savings account in a bank?

Options for Making Deposits

An important feature you need to consider with a savings account is the ease with which you can make deposits. The most comfortable accounts offer multiple deposit options. The deposit options available include ATM deposits, bank transfers, mail, and wire. Some banks also accept direct paycheck deposits into the account.

Compounding Period

When you receive the APY on an account, it consists of the interest rate and the compounding period. The compounding period of interest may be daily, monthly, or annually. The higher the frequency of compounding, the more profits you earn.

Access to Your Money

Once you put the money in the high-yield account, what options will be available for withdrawal? Will it support electronic funds transfer? Checks? Alternatively, ATM withdrawal?

Interest Rate

The main attractive feature of a high-yield savings account is the interest rate. It is the reason you have to confirm if the interest rate is a temporary or permanent rate. A temporary rate may be 'introductory' in the sense that it will change after a period. The permanent rate remains the same as long as you use the account.

Transaction Limit

In a month, an account may have a limit on the number of transfers or withdrawals you can perform.

Least Available Balance

Although there is an interest rate on the account, one of the conditions for earning the interest may be a minimum balance. Is there a minimum balance you need to know?

Opening and Maintenance Charges

Is there a cost of opening the account you desire? What about the maintenance cost for running the account?

With the maintenance costs, the bank may decide to charge a monthly, quarterly, or yearly levy. It is an amount that the bank charges to keep the account operational.

Additional Accounts

Under the conditions of gaining access to the high-yield savings account of individual banks, you will need to open another account with the bank. The account is commonly a checking account through which you will be able to access the funds in the savings account.

You need to analyze the effects of running an additional account in terms of the charges to determine if the savings account will be worthwhile.

How Much Can You Make from a High-Yield Account?

Depending on the APY on the high-yield savings account you open, the profits may vary for everyone. It is important to note that in most cases, you will get a higher APY with online banks. Nonetheless, a savings account is not usually the best for long-term investments.

Instead, use the account to keep your cash investments which will be enough to cover your expenses for a period. It should contain your emergency funds. A high-yield savings account should be a small part of your investment portfolio.

If you determine that $20,000 will be enough to cover your expenses for six months, you can save this amount in a high-yield savings account. So how much will you earn on a high-yield savings account when you compare it to a regular savings account?

Consider high-yield savings account offering a 2.35% APY with monthly compounding and a regular saving account offering a 0.05% APY with monthly compounding. With the high-yield savings account, you will have $20,475 at the end of the year while the regular savings account will increase to $20,010 in a year.

Money Market Accounts

Another type of savings accounts that banks offer is a money market account. Unlike a regular savings account, this account also has a higher interest rate. There are a few conditions for opening a money market account. These include a minimum balance which can be about a $1,000 for some banks but will usually vary.

Money market accounts usually allow up to three checks in a month like a checking account. There is also a limit to the monthly withdrawals on the account. Individuals may be limited to three withdrawals in a month depending on the bank where they open the account.

The Federal Deposit Insurance Corporation (FDIC) insures a money market account to prevent individuals from losing their money if the bank closes. The FDIC is a trustworthy government agency that has been able to limit losses within the banking institution.

Interest on Money Market Accounts

Money market accounts usually offer interest which is paid every month with daily compounding. Depending on the bank, the interest on the account will often differ. One of the significant reasons why the interest rates vary for each bank is due to competition. As a valuable customer, each bank is trying to attract more customers than the next. A higher interest rate is often the easiest way to achieve this goal.

With money market accounts, you can enjoy higher interest rates by having more money in the account. It is also important to note that opening a money market in a regular bank may not yield as much positive interest as with an online bank. With online banks, the low cost of operations is usually a major deciding factor in the high-interest rates.

Difference Between a Money Market Account and a Money Market Fund

It is common for people to confuse a money market account for a money market fund. Since the names are quite similar, it is understandable. Nonetheless, certain unique features differentiate these two instruments.

Like the deposit accounts which banks offer its customers, the FDIC also ensures a money market account. The insurance covers the up to $250,000 deposits in a single account.

A money market fund, on the other hand, is available through a broker. Since you are purchasing the fund from a broker, regulation of the fund is handled by the Securities and

Exchange Commission. The funds are commonly used in investing in cash equivalent securities and liquid cash.

Unlike the money market accounts, the rates on a money market fund may vary due to market movement and the Federal Reserve Rate. As a result, the price on the funds may sometimes be much lower than the rates on a money market account.

There are also various fees that investors must pay when operating a money market fund. These fees include transaction fees, expense ratios, and other charges. Accounting for the various fees that you must pay on a money market fund will often lead to a much lower return on investments.

A clear way to compare the money market account to the money market fund is through the returns which the broker offers and the interest rate from the bank. In most cases, since the interest rate on a money market account is usually higher, it is a much better alternative when you add the FDIC insurance on the account.

One area where the money market fund and the money market account are usually similar is the minimum balance to open. These instruments can have very high minimum balance requirements which the investor has to meet.

How Much Profits Can You Make on a Money Market Account?

If you operate a money market account with an APR of 2.5%, you can calculate the profits on the account.

The first step is to get the daily interest rate by dividing the APR by 365, and this is because the calculation of interests on money market accounts is usually done daily. In this case, the account will have a 0.007% daily interest.

If you deposit $100,000 in the account, the interest on the account will be $7 for the day. To get the interest for the next day, you will need to add the interest to the balance and calculate. It will be the ending balance for the previous day and starting balance for the new day.

You may need to do your calculations daily since there may be withdrawals and deposits in the account. It is also necessary to use updated rates in your calculations.

Certificate of Deposits (CD) Ladders

What is a Certificate of Deposit?

A certificate of deposit is also popularly referred to as a CD. As a banking investment tool, there are lots of similarities between a CD and a savings account. A significant difference between both tools is that while you can enjoy much higher interest rates on CDs, you will be unable to gain access to your money for a period.

The interest rate on a CD increases according to the length of the maturity date. More extended maturity date will offer higher interest on the CD.

The interest rate on a CD will be fixed from the time of purchase until the maturity date.

It is essential to understand that when using a CD, you are assuming that there will be no better interest rate during the period the CD will be open. In truth, it is possible for the interest rate on CDs to increase during this period. Nonetheless, you will be unable to enjoy this higher rate on an open CD.

Due to the uncertainty with investments, having a strategy is very important. When investing in CDs, an excellent approach to use is CD ladders.

It is a strategy that deals with the various issues affecting CDs. Using a CD ladder, you can quickly gain access to funds to benefit from the current higher interest rates.

What is a CD Ladder?

When you set up several CDs so that they have different maturity dates, it is known as a CD ladder. It gives you the option of spreading your money and provides an increase in the interest rate.

Why Should You Consider CD Ladders?

It is common for the CD rates to be higher when you put in more money or increase the duration of the CD. The interest rates on the CD may also rise while yours is already running which will prevent you from enjoying the new interest rates.

If you run a single CD, you may also have issues if you decide to withdraw the money earlier than the maturity date. There is usually a penalty for this action.

To avoid some of these issues a CD ladder can be a great option. Some of the benefits you can enjoy are as follows:

- You can choose the amount you wish to invest in each Certificate of Deposit.

- Instead of waiting for the maturity date of a single CD, you will be able to access your money more frequently at different times.

- In a situation where you have a CD maturing after each year, you can take advantage of the new rates when renewing the CD.

- Since you are now able to make long-term investments with the CDs, despite getting more various maturity dates, you can still enjoy the benefits of the higher rates.

How Do You Create a CD Ladder?

Creating a CD ladder can be quite easy. It all depends on the amount you intend to invest in CDs.

If as an investor, you are willing to invest $50,000 in CDs, then you can just split the funds. In this case, assume you are dividing the funds into five equal investments of $10,000 each. You can then create multiple CDs with varying maturity dates.

You can choose to create five CDs having maturity dates with six months intervals. Your

CDs will be as follows:

- $10,000 in a six-month CD

- $10,000 in a one-year CD

- $10,000 in an eighteen-month CD

- $10,000 in a two-year CD

- $10,000 in a thirty-month CD

The farthest maturity date in this CD ladder is thirty months. It implies that once the first CD reaches its maturity date, you can reinvest the funds in another CD with a thirty months maturity date. As a result, you will have one CD maturing every six months.

Is There Any Risk Associated With CD Investments?

The same as other investments, certain risks come with CD investments. The first risk that you need to consider is the limitation to the amount of growth you can get on a CD. It is due to the fixed interest rates that are available on CD investments. It means that if you have a one-year open CD with an interest rate of 1.5%, you will not get the benefits of an increase in the interest rate to 2%. The same also applies to a drop in the interest rate.

The possibility of a bank closing down is another risk that is common with a CD. If you are operating a CD ladder with a $300,000 total investment, you are likely going to lose some of your money if the bank shuts down. To avoid becoming a victim, it is crucial that you do not invest more than $250,000 in a single bank. It is the limit the FDIC insurance will cover. It would be best if you also understood that this limit includes funds in both your CDs and savings account in the same bank.

The liquidity of your funds is also another risk that is common with CDs. If there is an emergency and you require the funds in a CD, terminating the CD will result in a penalty. For this reason, it is crucial that you have both an emergency savings account as well as a CD ladder.

You can use a high-yield savings account also to make the most of the emergency savings.

Calculating the Interest on a CD Investment

Another key benefit of a CD investment is that the interest on it is compound interest. It means that the interest on the investment will grow much faster than with simple interest. The compounding period may be daily, monthly, or yearly depending on the issuing bank.

To calculate the CD at its maturity date; there is a simple formula you can use. You can also use an online calculator if this formula appears to be difficult. The formula is given below:

- $A = P(1 + r/n)^{(nt)}$

In the formula above,

- A is the total amount you will get at the CD maturity date

- Your initial investment is P

- The interest rate of the CD is r in decimal. An interest rate of 1.2% APY will be 0.012% in decimal

- n is the yearly compounding period of an investment. Although it is critical you verify the compounding period with your bank, a lot of CDs have a daily compounding. In a year, n = 365 with daily compounding

- The number of years till maturity date is the time, t

As an investor, consider a five-year CD with a $50,000 deposit, a 3% APR, and daily compounding.

To calculate the amount at the maturity date, we follow the formula to get the result below:

- A = 50,000 (1+0.03 / 365) ^ (365(5))

- A = 50,000 (1+0.000082191781) ^

(365(5))

- A = 50,000 (1.000082191781) ^ (365(5))

- A = 50,000 (1.000082191781) ^1825

- A = 50,000 (1.1618270815)

- A = 58091.354075

- A = 58091.35 when rounded off

If you can get a total of $58091.35 at the end of five years, it means your interest will be $8091.35.

It is crucial that you use the calculation in comparing the CDs from different banks before making a choice. It is also essential you are comparing it at the same level. The APY is not the same as the APR. The APR is usually lower than the APY. Using both in the same calculation will provide wrong results.

Chapter 7: Bonds

What Are Bonds

A bond is merely a form of a loan. In this case, the issuer of the bond is receiving credit from anyone that decides to purchase the bond. A bond issuer can be a corporation, municipalities, and governments.

In most cases where bonds are issued, it is often to meet the capital needs of the bond issuer. If as an investor, you decide to purchase a corporate bond, it merely implies that you are providing the corporation with a loan. The same also applies when you choose to buy a government bond.

Like other forms of investments, a bondholder is also entitled to interests on the loan they are giving to the bond issuer. In the context of bonds, the interest rate on a bond is referred to as the coupon. Maturity in bonds is time at which the bond issuer will repay the loan it received from the bondholder.

For example, if a corporation needs to raise $2 million in capital for a new project, it may decide to issue bonds. This decision makes the corporation the bond issuer in this case. The corporation may choose to sell 800 bonds at $2,500 per bond to its investors.

The maturity on the bonds may be four years while the annual interest on each bond is 5%. It means that the corporation is issuing four-year bonds with an annual coupon of 5%. At the end of four years, the corporation will pay off the $2 million principal.

With four years as the maturity of each bond, every bondholder will receive their initial $2,500 from the corporation which will amount to the $2 million. The $2,500 is known as the 'face value' of the bond.

A shorter maturity provides lower risks to the investors. Nonetheless, a longer maturity means that the interest on the bond will be much higher. So, you will be exposed to a higher risk to earn more returns on your investment.

A default or credit risk is also widespread with bonds. A default risk implies that there is a possibility that the bond issuer may be unable to repay the face value of the bonds at maturity.

To avoid investing in bonds that carry high default risks, there are Independent credit rating services whose main job is to assess the risk and interest rates that a bond offers its investors.

According to these assessments, bond issuers usually fall into one of two categories. There are those with a low credit rating and those with a high credit rating. Bond issuers with a high credit rating offer lower returns and lower risks. With an issuer having a low credit rating, you can expect to receive high returns in exchange for the high amount of risk you will have to bear.

Learning to Assess the Market Price of a Bond

There is always a unique method for quoting

prices on the various investment markets. The bond market also follows this unique trend.

In the bond market, a percentage of the face value of the bond is used in quoting the market price. A bond that has a market price of 95 implies that for a $1,000 face value, the market price of the bond is $950.

An easy method to follow is to add a zero to the market price to get a quick understanding. Trading at a discount is a situation where the face value exceeds the market price of the bond. It is trading at a premium if the market price is higher than the face value.

It is possible to find certain bonds that are trading at a price that is equal to the face value. Such a bond is trading at par value or simply trading at par.

The movement of interest rates also has a significant impact on bond prices. If the interest rates on bonds are currently dropping, it means that bondholders with older bonds will have a higher interest rate than the current bonds. It means that on the market, these bonds will be sold at a premium.

If the interest rates are on the rise, it means that the older bonds will have a lower interest rate. In this situation, the price of the older bonds will experience a fall.

The effects of an increase in interest rate or a fall in interest rate will vary depending on the length of the investment. If you are investing in short term bonds, falling interest rates will be more beneficial as you can sell the bonds at a higher price. On the other hand, an increase in the interest rate will mean that the bonds will be sold at a lower price.

With long term investments, a fall in interest rate will not affect the returns on the investment but reinvesting the returns will mean that you will be buying bonds with a lower interest rate. If the interest rates are increasing, you will have the opportunity to reinvest the returns in more profitable bonds with higher interest rates.

What is Duration?

Duration in bonds is a measure of the reaction of the bond prices if the interest rates change in any direction. It is merely a way to determine how much the price of a bond will change if there is a rise or fall in interest rates.

The face value of a bond and the coupon payment size are factors that affect the duration of a bond. The period of a bond is in years and is usually lower than the maturity of a bond.

Bond Investment Opportunities

Government Bonds

"Sovereign" debt, a debt type that is given by and receives support from a central government is one of the subcategories under the government bond sector. Some examples of sovereign government bonds include German Bunds, United States treasuries, Brazilian Government Bonds, U.K. Glits, Japanese Government Bonds

(JGBs), Government of Canada Bonds (GoCs) are some of the many sovereign government bonds available. Europe, Japan, and the United States over time have issued some of the most significant government bonds.

There are governments of certain countries that are also known for issuing sovereign bonds which have a link with inflation. This type of bond is called an inflation-linked bond. In the United States, it is known as Treasury Inflation-Protected Securities (TIPS). There is usually an adjustment of the interest and principal on a bond that is inflation-linked. It is done to show the changes which have taken place in the inflation rate. When done, this provides an inflation-adjusted return. Inflation-linked bonds are entirely different from other bonds. It is because they are very likely to experience more losses as long as standard rates are not as fast as interest rates.

Government bonds are not all about sovereign bonds. Apart from sovereign bonds, some of the other components that they include are:

Agency and "Quasi-Government" Bonds

There are lots of goals which are pursued by central governments. Some of these goals include building up small businesses and augmenting affordable housing. These are carried out through agencies which give out bonds to expand their operations. There are certain agencies with bonds that a central government guarantees while some others do not have a central government guaranteeing them. Huge organizations such as the European Investment Bank, the World Bank, etc., sometimes must get funds from the bond market for financing developments, as well as public projects.

Local Government Bonds

It is not a break from the norm for local governments to borrow funds to finance some of their projects. These projects might include building schools and bridges. There is an established local government bond market in the

United States. These types of bonds are called municipal bonds. Apart from local government bond markets, there are certain developed markets on which local government bonds are issued.

Municipal Bonds

Municipal bonds are sometimes called "munis." Several government agencies can issue these bonds. Included are local and state government agencies. Purchasing a government bond can be likened to lending the government some money.

One reason why a municipal bond is a fantastic investment is that federal taxes do not apply. If you are a resident in the state and city where you have your bonds, you can be sure that they will not also be taxed.

Usually, bonds get sold in increments of $5,000. It implies that you will have lots of fantastic tax benefits if you can invest this amount of money in bonds.

Corporate Bonds

When companies need to raise some funds for operations, they sometimes do this by issuing corporate bonds. Corporate bonds are not the same as stocks. They, therefore, should not be regarded as one. Stocks imply that you are a part owner of the company. However, buying bonds does not mean that you have any stake in the company. Nevertheless, when firms are about to go bankrupt, their bondholders get paid before stockholders get paid.

Only the bonds from the government sector beat a corporate bond. Over the years, they have been one of the most significant parts of the bond market. It is not a break from the norm for corporations to get money from the bond market when looking to get new businesses funded or increase their operations. In lots of developing countries and Europe, there is a rapid change taking place in the corporate sector.

There are two categories of corporate bonds.

These categories are speculative-grade which is sometimes called a junk bond or high-yield bond and investment grade. Firms which perform very highly are known to issue investment-grade corporate bonds. These firms get nothing less than a triple-B through agencies involved in credit rating. Firms with credit ratings that are considerably low can offer junk bonds or high-yield bonds. Although they come with an increased risk, their return on investment (ROI) is also high. Corporate bonds are proof that issuers financial health have significant differences.

One reason corporate bonds are agreeably more risky than municipal bonds is due to the higher tendency of a firm to fail to meet the demands of government agencies.

Relatively new companies and companies in sectors which are regarded as very competitive are known to issue speculative-grade bonds. In as much as a speculative-grade credit rating is an indication of a high probability of default, investors are compensated for the risk that they have to go through with the higher coupons which are associated with these bonds. When there is an improvement in fundamentals, ratings improve. Also, a deterioration in the credit quality of an issuer will lead to the downgrade of ratings.

Emerging Market Bonds

Federal governments of various countries as well as foreign companies also issue bonds. When the issuing party is an international company or developing country, the bond issued is an emerging market bond.

When developing nations give out corporate and sovereign bonds, these bonds are called emerging market (EM) bonds. There has been a development in the emerging market asset class since the 1990s. These developments have covered a vast variety of corporate, as well as government bonds which get issued in top foreign currencies. Included in these top currencies are the euro and the United States' dollar. Emerging market bonds have different countries as their source. As a result of this, their growth prospects are very different. With emerging market bonds, investment portfolios can be diversified. Also, risk-adjusted returns can be made available.

Although one trusted way to get your portfolio diversified is through the use of EM bonds, there could be risks posed by countries which do not have the same operations as the United States if you decide to make your decisions with absolutely fake or incomplete information.

If you have any interest in international and EM bonds, it is best to have a conversation with a broker with adequate experience with various countries and foreign firms. There is a very low tendency that the federal government will default. As a result of this, government bonds do not pose any risks. That, however, is not the case for international and EM bonds.

Mortgage-Backed Securities

Real estate and home loans offer these bond types. Unlike government bonds interest does not get paid two times a year. Instead, interest is paid every month.

When loans with similarities get pooled together, mortgage-backed securities are developed. Just like enterprises which are sponsored by the government, the MBS gets sold to agencies of the government. Firms such as investment banks or other private institutions are responsible for issuing these pools. Nonetheless, the United States government only back pools which get issued by government agencies.

If you have the right amount of cash to invest, then this is the right investment. The least amount that is needed for this investment is $10,000. A broker can help with the purchase of these securities.

Other Federal Government Bonds

All bonds come with some form of risk.

Nevertheless, risks by federal government bonds are some of the least. Federal government bonds are numerous. They include:

Treasury Bonds

Treasury bonds are fixed and long-term securities which are issued for the funding of budget deficits. State income taxes do not cover them, this is in addition to the fact that they are tied to interests after a period of six months. Nonetheless, with a maturity of 10 to 30 Years terms, the maturity of Treasury bonds is one of the longest.

Treasury Bills

These are known to last for less than one year. It, therefore, makes them short-term securities. It is possible to purchase them at a value which is considered to be much lower than its face value. You can also decide to convert them to cash when they are fully mature. Although treasury bills are not taxed at the state and local level, they are not exempt from federal government taxes.

Treasury Notes

Treasury notes last for a minimum of two years to s long as ten years. They involve an interest which has to be paid at six-month intervals. It continues until they attain full maturity. When the note is mature, the principal gets paid. Treasury notes have something in common with bills. They are free from local and state taxes. However, they are not free from federal taxes.

Treasury Inflation Protected Securities (Tips)

The principal on these securities are attuned in response to inflation, and the maturity can range from five to thirty years. Also, interest calculation uses depend on the inflated amounts.

Chapter 8: Commodities Investing

What Are Commodities

Any commercial product that is exchangeable for a similar type of product is known as a commodity. With different producers of a commodity, there may be slight differences in its quality, but there is still uniformity across the commodities. Most of the commodities available usually serve as raw materials in creating other services and products.

Generally, a commodity from one producer should be very similar to the same commodity from a different producer. It is the same way gold measurements are standardized all over the world. Some common commodities available include gold, oil, grains, and beef.

In commodities trading, the basis grade is an important feature that needs to be considered.

What is the Basis Grade?

For a commodity to be acceptable as a futures contract asset, it must meet a minimum standard. The minimum standard is the basis for the grade. It is also commonly referred to as a contract grade or par grade.

The importance of the basis grade is to ensure that the commodities traded on the market are uniform.

The basis grade serves as an essential benchmark for comparing commodities. If there are various producers exchanging copper metals on the market, it is crucial to assess the metals to determine its value on the market. The assessment is necessary since there will be minor differences in the production process of each producer.

If a product does not match up to the basis grade, it may be rejected since the quality is deemed to be undesirable. For a commodity on the market, there are some that sell at a higher value for the same quantity. It is often due to the commodity exceeding the basis grade. As the minimum standard, it is common for commodities to exceed this standard

A grading panel or qualified inspector usually assesses commodities. Any commodity that passes the assessment will receive a grading certificate that includes the grade of the commodity.

What is Commodity Investing

Commodity investing refers to investments in raw materials. The raw materials in question may be used directly or indirectly for different purposes. Commodities like food are usually consumed directly while other commodities like metals are necessary for other products to be manufactured.

Commodities investing involves trading in the commodities market. The movement of the market is usually dependent on the supply and demand of the products. The price of a commodity will go up if there is an increase in need with a decrease in the amount of the commodity. Similarly, a decline in demand with an increase in supply will result in a reduction of the price of a commodity.

For example, the supply of metals such as steel is usually in low supply due to the massive demand from countries that perform large-scale manufacturing like China. As a result of the small amount, there may be an increase in the price of steel for other countries seeking to make a purchase.

If you decide to invest in commodities, there are several options available. The investment options available for commodities usually include investing in Exchange Traded Funds (ETFs) for the commodity, investing in future contracts, purchasing the physical commodity, and other options.

Depending on your experience with the markets, it may be better to avoid some of the investment options available. It is a bold step to minimize fighting. Investing through a choice, you do not fully understand may result in massive losses.

Classification of Important Commodities

With so many commodities available on the market, classifying the commodities make them easier to assess. Below are the common classifications in use:

- Energy: This includes gasoline, crude oil, natural gas, and heating oil

- Agricultural produce: It consists of sugar, coffee, corn, rice, cotton, wheat, cocoa, and more

- Metals: copper, gold, silver, and platinum all fall within this group

- Livestock and Meat: Live cattle, lean hog,

feeder cattle, and pork bellies are included in this group

Benefits of Commodities Investment

There are different benefits that you get from investing in a commodity. Learning some of these benefits may attract you to this form of investment. They include:

A Means of Diversification

A key advantage that you can enjoy when investing in commodity stocks and commodities is the returns that differ from those available from bonds, stocks, and other investment instruments. By adding commodities investments to your portfolio, it is easier to minimize the effects of market volatility on your assets.

The Potential for Massive Returns

As stated earlier, the supply and demand of a commodity have a significant effect on its price. Other factors that affect the price include the economy, inflation, and exchange rates. If you are lucky to invest in commodities currently, there is a possibility of getting huge returns on investments. It is a result of the significant infrastructure projects ongoing in various countries around the world.

Companies that operate in the various commodities industry also benefit from the increase in the price of commodities. The rise in commodity prices has a direct effect on the price of company stocks.

Protection Against Inflation

The rapid drop in bonds and stock values is one of the adverse effects of inflation. In the case of commodities, inflation usually leads to an increase in the price of commodities. It means that you will benefit from owning commodities during periods of inflation.

Disadvantages of Commodities Investment

Just as there are advantages, there will always be

a few disadvantages of an investment. In commodities investing, these disadvantages include the following:

Risk of Losing Your Principal

Various factors affect the prices of commodities on the market. These factors include government regulations, competition between manufacturers around the world, import controls, economic conditions, and other significant world events. These factors have a great influence on the commodities industry and can also affect the volatility of prices.

If the effect on the market is severe, it is possible for your investments to lose their value and to sell these investments will result in the loss of your capital investments.

The Risks Associated With Foreign and Emerging Markets

When investing in an emerging market as well as a foreign market, there are a few factors that make the markets very volatile. In this case, it can be due to economic and political instability. The instability of the currency also affects.

Industry Limitations

In terms of your investment portfolio, you will be diversifying your portfolio by investing in commodities. Nonetheless, there are a few options available when it comes to investing in commodities. In most cases, commodities investment funds usually focus on one or two groups of commodities. As a result, price changes may have a significant impact on the value of the fund.

How to Invest in Commodities

Investing in Gold

Gold investments are one of the few investments opportunity that has remained popular over the years. Although it is a great investment option, it is essential that you understand what it entails before you decide to invest in gold. Your perspective will also influence your reason for this form of investment.

Before you decide to invest in gold, it is crucial that you understand the reason why you prefer gold investments. If you are blown away by the opportunity to store gold and then resell it later, you may need to rethink this option; this is a good option if there is an increase in gold price and you can resell it at a profit. Nonetheless, in this form of investment, you will be unable to earn interests or passive income from your gold investments.

If your goal is to create multiple investments that will provide an excellent cash flow, then there are other gold investment options that you can try out. There are Gold ETFs and shares in gold mining companies that yield profitable returns on your investments.

As a small investor, creating a steady cash flow is more important than holding money in storage. If you are hoping to guard against economic issues or inflation, then you can also invest in gold bullion.

How to Invest in Gold

Investing in Gold Mining Companies

Investing in gold mining companies involves buying into the shares the company has to offer. The value of the shares that a gold mining company provides will vary depending on the potential earnings of the company in the future and the price of gold on the market.

Since it is a mining company, there are a few factors you need to consider when purchasing stocks from gold mining companies. These include the reserves, hedging activities, production costs, management strategy, project development, and mine exploration.

There are several gold mining companies which are publicly traded, and they range from micro-cap companies to large-cap companies.

Gold Bullion

Gold bullion refers to gold that has very high purity. In most cases, it is gold with a minimum of 99.5% purity. The gold bullion is usually in the form of a gold ingot or gold bar. Gold bullion may either be a parted bullion or "unparted" bullion. Parted bullion refers to gold that doesn't contain any other metal and is in its purest form. The "unparted" bullion refers to gold that contains other metals.

One of the reasons why a lot of people still invest in gold bullion is because its price is beyond the control of the government. Only an increase or a decrease in the supply of gold will influence its price.

As an investment option, gold bullion is useful in protecting your money from losing value. Making profits by buying and reselling gold bullion will not yield the profits you desire. In most cases, individuals that own gold must resell at a wholesale price while the purchase of the gold bullion is in its retail price. Furthermore, this widens the spread between the ask and bid prices of gold bullion.

Gold ETFs

Gold exchange traded fund is one of the options available to investors who intend to own gold in paper form. As an investment option, a stock exchange usually supports the buying and selling of Gold ETFs. The primary asset here is gold.

In the case of Gold ETFs, investors have the benefit of purchasing at a price close to the actual value. Unlike with gold coins, jewelry, or bars, there are no additional charges due to the purchase or sale of the Gold ETF. Investors also enjoy transparency with the price of golds on the exchange market. To start trading Gold ETFs, investors will need a stockbroker to provide a trading account. In addition to the trading account, a demat account is also necessary. There is no limit to the amount of gold an investor can purchase with Gold ETFs. It can be as low as 1 gram. If an investor does not have enough funds to buy a lump sum, they can choose to use systematic investment plans that allow purchase at regular intervals.

There are three costs that investors have to cover when dealing with Gold ETFs. These include the broker cost, expense ratio, and tracking error. The broker cost comes up anytime the investor decides to sell or buy units of Gold ETFs. The expense ratio is the cost of fund management. Unlike the expense ratio with mutual funds, it is much cheaper. The tracking error is the costs that come up due to the cash holdings and fund expenses.

Gold Jewelry

Everyone that has an interest in gold investing will usually know about investing in gold jewelry. Most of the gold demand around the world is in the form of gold jewelry. In the case of gold jewelry, the unit of measurement is in karats.

The karat of gold jewelry is the measure of the

percentage of pure gold. The karat measurement starts at 10K to 24K with 24K representing pure gold. A 16K gold will represent 16 parts gold and eight parts other metals; for a 22K gold, it implies 22 parts gold and two parts other metal. Additionally, it represents a 91.7% gold jewelry.

The karat is a piece of relevant information that you must know when investing in gold jewelry. It influences both the durability and price of gold jewelry. In the case of gold jewelry, another factor that affects the price is the weight. The more a piece of gold jewelry weighs, the higher the worth of the jewelry.

Gold Options and Futures

Investing in gold options and futures is another investment option that may require a bit of experience and expertise. It is a speculative form of investment where you determine the price movement in either an up or down direction.

Investors can buy either a call or a put. Purchasing a call means that you are predicting an increase in price. If you are buying a call option for gold at say $100 for one year and the price increase to $800 within the year, your call option gives you the opportunity to pay the same $100 for gold worth $800 in the current market.

A put option means that you are predicting a drop in price. If you currently have gold options trading at $500 and you anticipate a fall in price in future, a put can help limit your losses.

Investing in Crude Oil

Crude oil also offers various investment options to the investor. Before deciding on what investment would be best, it is essential you carefully consider all the options available. Like gold investments, investors also have the option of investing in crude oil in its physical state. The only issue with this option is how to handle the physical commodity properly. If this option doesn't suit you, there are still various options that you can choose.

Regardless of the option you chose, it would help

if you understood that there would also be advantages as well as disadvantages. Below are some of the investment options available for individuals who prefer investing in energy:

Purchasing Physical Crude Oil

This method of investment may not be an option that is open to you as a beginner. Regardless, it is still available if you feel it would be worth the effort. In this form of investment, market prices of crude oil will affect the amount you will be able to sell your crude oil.

Other things you will need for this investment include storage facilities like a storage tank or a rail tank. Due to the volatility and toxic nature of crude oil, these unique storage facilities are a necessity. It would be best if you also thought of how you will be handling the crude oil.

Unless you are deciding to invest heavily into crude oil, buying it in its physical form will have more demerits which will outweigh the merits you stand to gain.

Crude Oil Futures Contracts

If you still want to work with the market prices of crude oil without having to thinks of handling and storage, then crude oil futures contracts offer a great form of investment. This form of crude oil investment is speculative. In this method of investment, you as an investor will decide on either buying or selling a crude oil futures contract.

Earning profits on the futures contracts depends on your ability to predict the price movement of crude oil at a particular time in future if you buy a contract, you are saying that at the expiration of the agreement, the price of crude oil will increase. If indeed there is an increase in price, then you profit on the contract. Price movement will imply a loss on the contract with the seller of the futures contract receiving the profit on this investment.

Investing in crude oil futures contracts also gives investors access to leverages. Leverage is merely a form of borrowed funds. Consider a case where a futures broker decides to allow you to purchase 500 barrels of crude oil. If you have just $3,000 in your futures brokerage account and 500 barrels is worth $30,000, then you are using leverage. In this case, the futures broker is offering you a margin of 10% of the contract value.

It is an excellent way to make massive profits with your small investment but can also result in massive losses.

Purchasing Stocks of Crude Oil Companies

What is a better way to invest in crude oil than investing in a company within the energy industry?

A company that deals in the exploration, production, refining, transportation and sales of crude oil offer great options for investing. The rise and fall of crude oil prices usually affect companies dealing in crude oil exploration and production. The value of these companies usually increases and decreases in response.

This increase in value is only for the exploration and production companies. These changes in crude oil prices do not usually influence other companies that require crude oil as an input for manufacturing other products. In the case of a refinery, there may be a loss of profits due to the increase in crude oil prices without an increase in prices of refined products.

Investing in Base Metals

What Are Base Metals

Any metal that will corrode or oxidize with ease on exposure to moisture or air is referred to as a base metal. These metals are essential commodities that are useful for industrial and commercial purposes like manufacturing and construction. Other crucial features of these metals include their abundance in nature and the ease of the mining process to get the metals.

A much simpler definition of base metals is metals that do not contain iron. The non-ferrous metals. Nickel, zinc, lead, copper, aluminum and tin fall within this category.

Regardless of the availability, ease of access, and relatively low price in comparison to precious metals, the base metals still hold a significant position within the global economy.

Using copper as an example, many economists use the price of this metal in determining how well the global economy is faring. That said, this is due to its rapid price response to economic trends on a worldwide scale. Since it is an important construction material, an economic forecast in which a fall in the price of copper indicates a decrease in economic activity in the home construction sector of the economy. An increase in the price of copper will also mean growth in economic activity.

There are also lots of infrastructures that depend on the base metals. Without base metals like nickel, it would be impossible to obtain stainless steel.

Base Metals Futures Contracts

Trading of base metals is widespread around the world. The London Metals Exchange (LME) provides a large number of base metal trades around the world. Investors can also find various exchanges that will provide base metals futures contracts.

There are other options for investing in base metals including:

- Investing in base metal ETFs

- Investing in base metal companies

Chapter 9: Peer-to-Peer Lending

What is Peer-To-Peer Lending (P2P)?

With peer-to-peer (p2p) lending, individuals can borrow money they need without having to depend on any recognized financial institution as a middle man. Peer-to-peer lending involves an increase in time spent, potential risks and efforts than the regular form of lending and borrowing. It is a result of eliminating the middleman. P2P lending is a form of credit which is sometimes called crowdlending or social lending.

The traditional way of applying for a loan by small businesses and individuals is through the application for bank loans. When individuals ask for a bank loan, the bank goes ahead to carry out lots of reviews on the credit history of the applicant. The aim of doing this is to assess the ability of an individual to repay the loan they intend to receive from the bank. If the applicant is qualified to get a loan, the interest rate which should be charged is determined. As an individual, if you do not want to pay high interest rates for a loan or if you know you do not qualify for a bank loan, you can decide to make use of peer-to-peer lending.

Peer-to-peer lending involves borrowers getting loans from investors that are ready to release funds with an interest rate which is generally agreed on. Peer-to-peer lending is quite risky. As a result of this, the investor has to go through the profile of the borrower before lending them money. It is possible because the profile of the borrower can be accessed on a peer-to-peer platform. A borrower sometimes gets a fraction of their request from a single investor while others may get the full amount. If a borrower receives only a part of the amount asked for from an investor, other investors on the peer-to-peer platform can fund the borrower's request. Now, since there are multiple sources for the loan, a borrower will have to refund to all sources monthly.

On peer-to-peer platforms, borrowers can link up with investors with interest rates that are not scary. Borrowers make money from the peer-to-peer platform because loans given out bring money in through interests. This interest which an investor gets from a borrower sometimes exceeds the amount they can earn from other investments like the stock market. Peer-to-peer lending also makes it easy for borrowers to have access to funds that they would have found it very difficult to access if they were to go through the traditional means of getting a loan. That is not all. Also, the interest rate that is attached to credit is more beneficial to a borrower than what a bank offers.

P2P lending is a process which gives an individual the freedom to lend or borrow funds without having to pass through the general process that individuals in need of funds have to go through. It involves getting money from other sources other than financial institutions.

P2P investing unlike P2P lending involves playing the role of an investor in the entire process of getting a loan.

How Can I Find the Right Company to Invest in?

It is one thing to have an understanding of what P2P lending and investing are and another thing to know how to go about it the P2P lending and investment the right way. By now, you are probably thinking about the right firm to invest with.

Everyone that has ever needed to raise funds through the peer-to-peer lending can attest to the fact that it is of utmost importance to locate a trustworthy and reputable investment platform. Even, this should come first on your scale of preference. Although there are lots of sites dedicated to online investment, it is vital that you carry out adequate research before committing to any.

The best company for you to pay money into should:

- Come with a high return for every investment. It is quite apparent as the primary aim of putting money into P2P loans is to make some extra money. Different firms have different returns on investment. Regardless of this, it would help if you were on the lookout for firms with return on investment which is not less than 10-12 percent.

- Should offer a smooth, rapid, and easy process which features a reliable financing system and a user-friendly platform.

- Come with a BuyBack guarantee and keep your money protected. Sometimes, unexpected situations come up. Well, if you can always access your money quickly, you will not have so many problems.

- Keep investors protected from borrowers

that pay late. It implies that there should be a guarantee that the company will settle the investor if there is a default on payments by the borrower.

How Does P2P Investing Work?

Investing in P2P is a simple process. As soon as you get a P2P platform that you are interested in investing in, the next step is to become an investor or lender. Likewise, this is followed by the amount you are interested in lending and how long you intend lending. Once done, you can go on to fund your account and begin investing. It is normal for lots of P2P firms to keep your funds for a period which will be agreed on. So, to take part in P2P lending, you should be ready to stay away from your money for a certain period.

There are firms which offer a BuyBack guarantee. One of such financing firms is Fast Invest. With a BuyBack guarantee, you can decide to quit as an investor whenever you need to. The implication of this is that it is possible to pull out your investments when the occasion demands.

You are probably wondering how P2P firms can guarantee that those you lend money to will pay back.

Although the P2P platform is different from the process of getting money from traditional financial institutions, it still has a way of screening borrowers. As soon as a loan gets approved, borrowers can access the money that they asked for. They will, however, have to pay some amount together with interests every month.

As far as alternative financing is concerned, the process of loan verification is carried out by lending partners with the right license and are known to finance other financing platforms.

After this is a meticulous check which then platform does by itself. It is a way of getting the risk evaluated. It is also done to ensure that borrowers make payments as at when due.

Advantages and Risks of Lending

Peer-to-peer lending offers a massive chance of passive income. It is also, a good return on investment. The above are only a few of the most significant benefits of taking part in peer-to-peer lending. Additionally:

- Peer-to-peer lending needs little upfront capital in exchange for a reasonably good return. All things being equal, a yield of 4.4% is made by P2P lenders averagely. It is way better than trying to make money from a savings account.

- Peer-to-peer lending has downsides. One of its disadvantages is the fact that the involves risks which are usually bigger than industry experts make the public aware of. There is an increase in the rate of delinquency of peer-to-peer lenders.

Unfortunately, there is no real structure against delinquency. It is one reason a higher return is associated with very risky loans.

Depending on your initial investment and considering charges on the platform, you can earn over $20,000 annually as a P2P investor. The ROI percentage also matters a lot.

Chapter 10: Conclusion

If you are currently on this final chapter, then I expect you have taken note of some of the main points throughout the book up to this point. These are some of the most significant bits of information that will aid you in achieving your investing goals.

As a way to get started, reading this book should have given you an idea of what investing covers and some of the main reasons why you need to start investing. You also learned about some of the necessary steps you need to take if you want to be successful as an investor.

To reach my goal of telling you about 31 investment opportunities you can get into, the stock markets provided five of these opportunities. Although the stock market is vast and consists of big-time market players, there is always room for any individual willing to put their skills and knowledge to work.

The investment funds also opened four unique opportunities for investment. It is a necessary investment option which grants you access to investments which generally would require a massive amount of capital. Through investment funds, all you need to do is add a small part of the money while there will be other investors like you that will complete the other parts.

If you need a to drop into a more familiar scene, then real estate investments also offer great opportunities. Most of the investment opportunities in this category are easy to understand. Real estate investments are also straightforward to get into.

For the investor that has much time for self-development, forex trading is another option that offers boundless opportunities to make profits. It isn't all sweet with forex trading, but once you get the hang of this investment, you will reap massive rewards.

From saving a part of your monthly allowance to

using traditional banking services, investing in banks is quite easy for many people. If you knew about savings as the only form of banking investments, then you must have been shell-shocked to learn about CDs and CD ladders. Don't waste time dwelling; take advantage of this opportunity now.

Bonds are another common form of investments that a lot of people hear about from time to time. Investing in bonds is not as difficult as you think, think of it as lending money to those in need.

Commodities investing is just like investing in the stock markets. You are buying commodities with the belief that there will either be a rise in price or a decrease in price. Commodities investing can also be a great way to protect yourself from the effects of inflation.

The last investment opportunity is the peer-to-peer lending which is becoming popular. It is an excellent option for people that do not have access to traditional bank loans. What better way to get money when all other options prove abortive?

As promised, I have provided 31 investment opportunities from which you can make a steady income if you use the right strategies. Nonetheless, this book will not be complete without listing a few other possibilities. These can generate a steady income but may sometimes require a significant amount of time.

Other Sources of Passive Income That Require Time Investment

Most of the investment opportunities discussed in this book usually require a lot of money investments. Other profitable investment ideas may need a lot of time investment and little or no money investments. The following are some of these investments:

Blogging

Making money as a blogger remains one of the best sources of passive income for many people.

Starting a blog is quite easy and requires very little monetary investment. The primary requirement is your time and a lot of high-quality contents.

If you can post relevant, high-quality content on your blog consistently, it will grow to be very popular. The popularity of your blog will attract more traffic. So, this is your reason for starting the blog.

As your blog continues to attract visitors, you can monetize the blog by either running an affiliate program or through advertising. Since you are getting, a lot of traffic on your blog, you may get offers from individual companies that want you to advertise their product to your readers.

You can also incorporate Google AdSense on your blog. Through ads on your blog that are placed by Google, you can generate a steady income stream.

For those who don't have the time to build up a blog, then buying a blog is another option. If you find a blog with decent traffic that seems abandoned, you can try buying it from the owner. Some blog owners may decide to sell if they do not have enough time to operate the blog anymore.

Blog prices can be very high, and the prices usually depend on the monthly income of the blog. It is crucial you search for a blog that has content that will remain relevant even when it is not in operation for an extended period.

Adding new high-quality content will also increase the monthly income of such blog sites. There are various places you can buy a blog, and one of the popular marketplaces is Flippa. Some blogs can provide up to $3,000 in yearly income.

Creating an eBook

Publishing an eBook has become a great way to generate income for many individuals. Many people engage in self-publishing of eBooks to earn significant passive income. A lot of self-published books are available on Amazon with a lot of people purchasing these eBooks.

If you decide to create an eBook, you should have a topic you are passionate about that the eBook will cover. Editing the eBook is the next step after writing. You can then use Amazon's Kindle Direct Publishing or any other relevant program to publish the eBook.

Making money from eBooks requires patience. Marketing is also essential if you are to make money creating eBooks.

Investing in a Business

Investing in a business doesn't always have to be through buying shares or bonds. You can decide to buy a growing business or become a quiet investor in the company.

When you decide to buy a business, you are not looking for a company that will require much input from you. The business should already be stable enough to operate without any external influence.

If buying a business seems like too much work, you can just become an investor in a company. Being a quiet partner in business can yield high returns but may also involve high risks. You can do this by lending money to businesses through some of the tools available for this purpose.

Affiliate Marketing

Affiliate marketing works well if you have a blog or a website that generates a high amount of traffic. Your site will become a goldmine for companies looking to reach more potential clients. You will earn a commission by becoming an affiliate marketer for any company.

It will also require patience on your part, so don't think of it as a scheme to get-rich-quick. Your income may come as a flat fee or as a percentage of the profits made from sales linked to your site. There are dedicated websites that provide offers for affiliate programs. Visit any of these sites to find an offer that will suit you best.

Renting Out a Car

Many people usually need a car to rent. These can be individuals visiting your city for the first time or anyone just looking to get around. If you have a car you don't often use, renting it out can be more beneficial than having it parked idle.

Some sites allow you to list your car for rent. Once the car is registered, these platforms will handle all the other processes. In return, you earn passive income through the listing.

Your location and the type of car you are listing can sometimes have a significant impact on the passive income it generates.

Renting Out Space in Your House

If you don't have much money for large scale real estate investments, then you can make use of what you have at your disposal. You can list a room in your house on sites like Airbnb or VRBO. It is an effortless way to earn passive income in a single place.

Airbnb Listing

When people are traveling around the world, they sometimes want cheaper accommodation. Using Airbnb provides access to accommodations that meet their requirements and are also within their budget.

On the Airbnb platform, listings are separated into an entire home, shared room, or private room. It all depends on what you have to offer. There is a commission of 3% that Airbnb receives as payment for their services anytime you get a booking.

VRBO Listing

Similar to Airbnb, VRBO covers large rental properties. It has a database that includes more than 2 million rental properties available.

For individuals who want to set-up their property for rent all through the year, VRBO charges an annual fee. It is also effortless to list your property on the platform.

If you hope to get more people to rent your space or property, you need to get lots of positive reviews.

Investment Principles That Should Guide You

Becoming an investor is not a get-rich-quick scheme through which you can make money just because you want to. You need to follow strategies as we discussed earlier and have many principles guiding your investments.

Following the principles below will help you as a beginner, and along the way, you will also develop other policies that will be unique to your investment style. The principles below have been of immense help during my growth as an investor:

Diversify Your Investments

Any successful investor you meet will always mention diversification as one of their main reasons for success. It is a principle you must not overlook. By diversifying your investments, you are spreading your investment capital across various investment opportunities. It protects you from losing all your money if one of your investment fails.

Allocate Assets Effectively

The returns on your investment depend primarily on how you allocate your assets. Allocation of assets should be a priority when diversifying your investments. It is essential that you build up an excellent strategy for allocating your resources to avoid investing a large amount of your capital in an asset that is currently overvalued with little long-term benefits.

Improve Your Knowledge on Returns and Risk

To be successful as an investor, you need to understand the relationship between risk and returns. Various investment opportunities have a different level of risk. With most investments, a higher risk often has a high yield.

Regardless of the returns, it would help if you only choose an investment with a risk level you are comfortable handling. If the risk is too high, you may suffer significant setbacks if you lose on the investments. How will you handle such delays? People treat setbacks differently. Some investors have substantial investment capital that will cover any significant setback.

As a beginner, taking an investment with a very high risk means losing all your capital if you make the wrong choice.

Choose Long Term Investments

You will not be making the most of any investment opportunity if your strategy is to continue moving in and out of the investment market. There are specific growth opportunities that are only open for a few days on certain investments. It would be best if you had long term investments to make the most of these growth opportunities.

Take Advantage of Compounding

Compounding is an important concept that can mainly increase your returns on investment. Understanding how compounding works will be helpful when selecting the best investment opportunity on the market. Compounding can also affect your effects negatively on what is known as reverse compounding.

The higher the capital you lose, the more difficult it becomes to reach a breakeven point.

Reinvest

The easiest way to grow your investment portfolio is to reinvest your dividends. Re-investing will give you opportunities to gain higher returns on investment with the ability to tap into increasing interest rates on various investments.

A Margin of Safety is Necessary

Investing with a margin of safety means that you are buying an asset or securities at a price that is lower than its actual worth. It reduces the risk of your investment.

Another benefit of having a margin of safety is that you can earn more on investment as soon as the value of the investment begins to appreciate. You should always consider an investment with unfavorable conditions in mind.

Prepare for Market Volatility

Volatility in investments can appear in the form of portfolio volatility and market volatility. Unlike portfolio volatility which is controllable, market volatility is beyond the control of any individual investor.

Since it is not within your control, your best option is to prepare for market volatility and use it to make the most of available investment opportunities.

Dedicate Yourself to an Investing Strategy

If you are going into investing without a plan, you will lose all your capital before you can make any progress. An investing strategy encompasses all the areas that define how you operate.

Do you prefer value investing or growth investing, do you prefer bonds to stocks? Alternatively, are you after long-term or short-term investments?

Building an investment strategy that will work excellently for your investment style will require you to assess all these critical areas. Following this strategy will result in consistency in your approach towards any investment opportunity. As a value investor, jumping onto a growth investment opportunity may result in losses you will not comprehend.

Incorporate Strategies for Risk Management

Risk management strategies are essential in controlling portfolio volatility. Your inability to control the volatility of your portfolio will have a significant impact on the returns of your investments. Risk control is beneficial in surviving the effects of a bear market.

My Final Words to You

Investing your money for the long-term benefits may seem difficult considering you will be depriving yourself of the luxurious lifestyle you can afford at this moment. Regardless, it is a step you need to take if you want to live a life of comfort. Working to make money will not always be an option.

Taking advantage of the boundless opportunities available to you is a step you must take now. If you keep procrastinating, you will never get started. Remember, there is no time like the present.

If you have learned a lot from this book and would like others to find this book with ease, do leave a review. Thank you and have a good time making money from your investments.

Bibliography

6 Best Ways to Invest in Gold With Little Money | ProfitableVenture. (2019). Retrieved from https://www.profitableventure.com/investing-gold-for-beginners/

18 ways technology has changed investing | Stacker. (2019). Retrieved from https://thestacker.com/stories/205/18-ways-technology-has-changed-investing

Advantages & Disadvantages of Money Market Accounts. (2019). Retrieved from https://finance.zacks.com/advantages-disadvantages-money-market-accounts-2170.html

APY Interest Calculator | Calculate APY Rate | Axos Bank. (2019). Retrieved from https://www.axosbank.com/Tools/Calculators/APY-Calculator

Backman, M. (2019). Should I Start a CD Ladder? -- The Motley Fool. Retrieved from https://www.fool.com/retirement/2017/05/19/should-i-start-a-cd-ladder.aspx

Base Metals. (2019). Retrieved from https://www.investopedia.com/terms/b/base-metals.asp

Bethell, A. (2019). How to Wholesale Real Estate the Right Way. Retrieved from https://fitsmallbusiness.com/how-to-wholesale-real-estate/

Bullion. (2019). Retrieved from https://www.investopedia.com/terms/b/bullion.asp

Caplinger, D. (2019). Your Complete REIT ETF Guide -- The Motley Fool. Retrieved from https://www.fool.com/investing/2019/01/04/your-complete-reit-etf-guide.aspx

Diddy, P., Diddy, P., Pip, H., Pipslow, D., Pip, H., & Pip, H. et al. (2019). Learn Forex Trading With BabyPips.com. Retrieved from https://www.babypips.com/

Fiorillo, S. (2019). How to Invest in Real Estate: Buying vs. Not Buying Property. Retrieved from https://www.thestreet.com/how-to/invest-in-real-estate-14735368

Gitlen, J. (2019). How Much Do House Flippers Make? - LendEDU. Retrieved from https://lendedu.com/blog/much-house-flippers-make/

Guidotti, D. (2019). Types of Bank Investments | MMA | CD | IRA | Bonds | 401K. Retrieved from http://www.pfhub.com/bank-investments-for-smart-investors/

How Dividends Work | dummies.com. (2019). Retrieved from https://www.dummies.com/personal-finance/investing/online-investing/how-dividends-work/

How do Mutual Funds Work - I Will Teach You To Be Rich. (2019). Retrieved from https://www.iwillteachyoutoberich.com/blog/all-about-mutual-funds/

How Investing in Cannabis Works - Marijuana Stocks | Cannabis Investments and News. Roots of a Budding Industry.™. (2019). Retrieved from https://marijuanastocks.com/how-investing-in-cannabis-works/

How to Invest in Real Estate: The Basics | Resources. (2019). Retrieved from https://fundrise.com/education/blog-posts/how-to-invest-in-real-estate-the-basics

Investing for Beginners. (2019). Retrieved from https://www.thebalance.com/investing-for-beginners-4074004

Kirkpatrick, D. (2019). Renting vs. Buying: The True Cost of Home Ownership - Can I Retire Yet?. Retrieved from https://www.caniretireyet.com/renting-vs-buying-true-cost-home-ownership/

Market Capitalization: Large Cap, Mid Cap & Small Cap Stocks. (2019). Retrieved from https://financialengines.com/education-center/small-large-mid-caps-market-capitalization/

Marketable Securities. (2019). Retrieved from https://www.investopedia.com/terms/m/market ablesecurities.asp

Peer-to-peer lending explained | Lending Works. (2019). Retrieved from https://www.lendingworks.co.uk/blog/peer-to-peer/peer-peer-lending-explained

Samurai, F. (2019). Ranking The Best Passive Income Investments. Retrieved from https://www.financialsamurai.com/ranking-the-best-passive-income-investments/

Stock Investment Strategies - Corporate Finance Institute. (2019). Retrieved from https://corporatefinanceinstitute.com/resources/knowledge/trading-investing/stock-investment-strategies/

The Anatomy of Trading Breakouts. (2019). Retrieved from https://www.investopedia.com/articles/trading/

08/trading-breakouts.asp

Types of Investments | FINRA.org. (2019). Retrieved from http://www.finra.org/investors/types-investments

Underlying Asset Definition. (2019). Retrieved from https://www.investopedia.com/terms/u/underlying-asset.asp

What are Penny Stocks and How Do They Work? - Wall Street Survivor. (2019). Retrieved from https://www.wallstreetsurvivor.com/starter-guides/what-are-penny-stocks-how-they-work/

What Are the Advantages & Disadvantages of Investing in a Bank Account?. (2019). Retrieved from https://finance.zacks.com/advantages-disadvantages-investing-bank-account-4394.html

What are the different types of investments?. (2019). Retrieved from https://www.commsec.com.au/support/learn/investing-basics/what-are-the-different-types-of-investments.html

What Is a Hedge Fund? - dummies. (2019). Retrieved from https://www.dummies.com/personal-finance/investing/what-is-a-hedge-fund/

Zinn, D. (2019). Everything You Need To Know About Bonds | Bankrate.com. Retrieved from https://www.bankrate.com/investing/investing-in-bonds/